Hilarious Skits for Youth Ministry

by Chris Chapman

Group
Loveland, Colorado

Dedication

For Susan, my wife, who raced 'round madly with four children while all this was being typed up.

Note: The price of this text includes the right for you to make as many copies of the skits as you need for your immediate church performing group. If another church or organization wants copies of these skits, it must purchase *Hilarious Skits for Youth Ministry* in order to receive performance rights.

Hilarious Skits for Youth Ministry

Copyright © 1998 Chris Chapman

First Printing

Credits
Book Acquisitions Editor: Amy Simpson
Editor: Candace McMahan
Chief Creative Officer: Joani Schultz
Copy Editor: Janis Sampson
Art Director: Ray Tollison
Cover Art Director: Jeff A. Storm
Cover Designer: Diana Walters
Computer Graphic Artist: Joyce Douglas
Photographer: Jafe Parsons
Production Manager: Gingar Kunkel

Library of Congress Cataloging-in-Publication Data
Chapman, Chris, 1957-
   Hilarious skits for youth ministry / by Chris Chapman.
      p.   cm.
   Summary: A collection of eight humorous skits centered around theological and biblical issues.
   ISBN 0-7644-2033-X
   1. Drama in Christian education. 2. Church work with teenagers. 3. Amateur plays.
[1. Christian life--Drama. 2. Plays.]
   I. Title.
   BV1534.4.C48   1998
   246' .72--dc21   97-41641
                                                        CIP
                                                          AC

10 9 8 7 6 5 4 3 2 1   07 06 05 04 03 02 01 00 99 98
Printed in the United States of America.

Contents

Introduction

Hello. Let's be perfectly honest right from the start!

You're probably a youth group leader or some such busy person with limited time. You need time-consuming verbiage and guff like you need a hole in the head. Therefore, you don't want to have to read a lengthy, deeply theological introduction as you decide how to use this book. So goodbye to highbrow philosophical language and in-depth psychological analysis. Here is a concise introduction.

1. Contents of book (i.e., "What's in it?")—Skits, eight of them. All center around theological and biblical issues, themes, characters, and incidents that youth fellowship, Bible study, and discussion groups deal with and ask questions about.

2. Nature of dramas (i.e., "What type of skits?")—Comedy, relatively compact (about five to fifteen minutes), yet with enough pith and guts to challenge someone who wants to "get into a bit of drama." Note: The dramas don't necessarily require funding from the World Bank. Most can be staged effectively with virtually no props, sets, or costumes if you don't want to do a large-scale production. The dramas offer everything from good-sized speaking parts to "race on, race off" nonspeaking roles. In other words, everyone in the group can participate without being intimidated by having to learn a lot of lines. You can therefore include all your youth group members, even little Tommy, whose mother is sure he has a big future on the stage but who actually gets scared spitless every time he has to appear before himself in the mirror.

3. Suggested uses for skits (i.e., "What do I do with them?")—The range is endless. Why not consider using them as discussion starters before studying material relevant to the skit? The humor and fun of the skits help open young minds to the possibilities of the themes which can be drawn from the skits. What about using them to reinforce material your group has *already* dealt with? Study the relevant section of the Bible first, discuss it, expand on it, and then do the skit as a fun-filled culminating activity. The increased understanding of the relevant material and themes will lead to greater appreciation of the humor. And that's not all. Your kids could read the skits for pleasure; perform them for fellowship or study groups; perform them in concerts, church services, group meetings, coffee shops, and camps; or just have fun with them. (This latter seems trivial, but in tandem with the other uses, it helps to dispel the widespread delusion that church, the Bible, and Christianity are boring.) All of these uses help to encourage humor and fun in fellowship and church meetings, which makes members feel "safe" in inviting non-Christian friends to them.

4. Guarantee of skits' effectiveness (i.e., "What reaction will they get?")—Be assured: These skits have all been road-tested in front of an audience of hundreds ranging from fourteen-year-olds to adults. They received thunderous responses—of the positive type. Numerous audience members of all ages related how the skits had helped them in their understanding of certain issues, situations, characters, and questions. Requests for more were common.

5. Additional free accessories (i.e., "What's in it for me?")—Yes, my friends (and I do mean my friends), you get, not only this bumper harvest of quality skits, but also, absolutely free: a glossary of stage terms; outstanding suggestions of how to use each specific drama for youth group activities, discussions, and extensions; Scripture links; user-friendly lists of props, costumes, characters, and other necessaries to make it easier for you to put the skits on the boards; specific suggestions on how to set up stage, scenery, and sound effects; and an assortment of "cues" to help you stage the skits.

6. Author's recommendation—With all this, how can you resist? I might have to get a few copies myself!

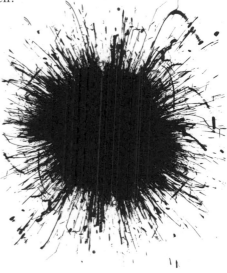

Glossary of Frightening Stage-Type Terms

Now, as you read these scripts, you will find that there are various abbreviations in the stage directions—DSC, USL, and CS, for example. If you aren't already familiar with these terms, don't worry. They are fairly easy to understand once you've had them explained.

They are just descriptions of various parts of the stage, and they help you space your actors out, place props and sets, and visualize the stage as you read the script.

The first thing to remember is that all the directions are from the actors' point of view. Therefore SR (Stage Right) is the right-hand half of the stage seen from where the actor is standing. (From the audience's point of view, it is the left-hand side of the stage, and this is where some confusion can occur.) Thus SR is Stage Right and SL is, obviously, Stage Left. US (Upstage) is the "back of the stage"—away from the audience. DS (Downstage) is the front, and CS (Center Stage) is smack in the middle of the whole thing. These directions divide the stage into four quarters with CS being where the dividing lines cross.

All the variations stem from these five starting points. For example, when you combine US with SR, you get USR (Upstage Right) which is (from the actors' point of view) "the back of the stage on the right-hand side." DSL, therefore, is the opposite corner. From the actors' point of view, DSL is "the front of the stage on the left-hand side." DSC is Downstage Center, the most obvious place on the whole stage (i.e., not where you put little Tommy who faints in front of the mirror).

With these directions and a little practice, you can give smooth, standardized directions to the actors and technical crew about exactly where you want things to happen. It avoids the old problem of the director shouting, "Can you come up a bit and go to the right?" to which the actor replies, "Whose right and what do you mean 'up'?"

It really is worthwhile spending a bit of time getting these stage directions firmly in the heads of your kids. It may take a little time at first, but it will save you a lot of time later. The whole process can be made a little more interesting by talking the directions through with your kids and especially by giving them the diagram (p. 7) with the relevant directions written on it (USL, CSL, DSL, USC, CS, DSC, USR, CSR, DSR).

You can then play a little game with them to help them remember. They all get on stage, and you yell a direction. They all have to race to that part of the stage. When they become bored with that, you can pick a couple of monitors who have strong fingers. Then you call out directions, the group members rush to the right place, and the monitors have lots of fun frantically tickling anyone who isn't in the right section quickly enough. (Remember to do it in Christian love. Discussion after this activity can deal with forgiveness and the concept of revenge belonging to the Lord.)

Stage Terms

Abbreviated Stage Terms

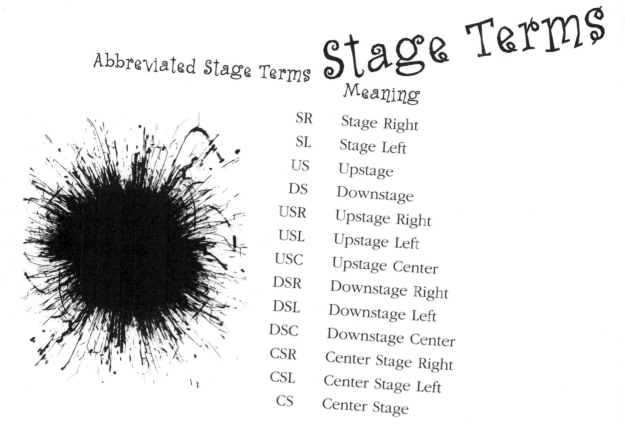

Abbreviated Stage Terms	Meaning
SR	Stage Right
SL	Stage Left
US	Upstage
DS	Downstage
USR	Upstage Right
USL	Upstage Left
USC	Upstage Center
DSR	Downstage Right
DSL	Downstage Left
DSC	Downstage Center
CSR	Center Stage Right
CSL	Center Stage Left
CS	Center Stage

Laid out on a rectangular stage, they look like this:

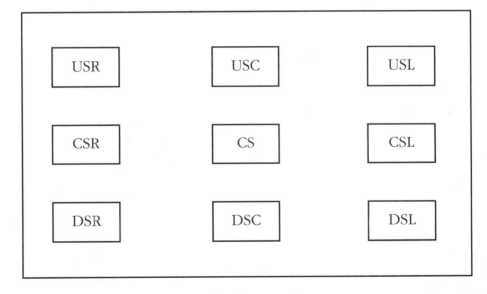

Audience

OOOOOOOOOOOOOOOOOOOOOOOOOOOOOOOOOOOO
OOOOOOOOOOOOOOOOOOOOOOOOOOOOOOOOOOOOOO
OOOOOOOOOOOOOOOOOOOOOOOOOOOOOOOOOOOOOO

The Genesis Home Movie

Themes: Creation, sin, the Fall, redemption, God's plan of salvation

Summary: Dr. Archetype of the British Museum's archaeology section has uncovered an ancient box which actually contains God's own home-movie footage of the events in the book of Genesis—all silent and in fast motion, of course.

Scripture Link: Genesis

Discussion Ideas: Genesis is a long and hefty book with a lot happening in it. For this reason, and because of the general biblical illiteracy that is rife today, many people—even churchgoers—are confused about Jacob and Esau, when Noah arrived on the scene, and who it was who was nearly sacrificed by his father. This skit gives an effective overview of the whole thing. Because it is done in fast motion, it is even funnier and more compact. It gives a good running summary of the main characters, their relationships and adventures, and the overall themes of the first book of the Old Testament.

Discussion may center around God's creation of the world; the effects of sin and the Fall; the beginnings of God's work of redemption, especially his choice of certain people and families to be his own special people; and his consequent working in their lives.

Props and Costumes: Many and varied, but fairly easy to assemble. Costumes may be very basic, consisting mostly of tea towels tied around heads and bedsheets draped around bodies. Particular costumes, such as Jacob's hairy coat and Cain's and Abel's outfits, can be easily assembled using sheepskin car seat covers or sheepskin baby blankets. You will also need wire-frame paper wings for the four angels; a small box; an ax, sword, or similar sharp object; a big club; a small bow-and-arrow set; a sword for Gabriel; a colorful coat for Joseph; and some confetti. In addition, you will need to create green paper fig leaves; cardboard cutouts of Dust Specs (brown blobs); a cardboard cutout of a moth; a large poster with "Focus" written blurrily on one side and clearly on the other; and large posters with the numbers one to five written separately on each. You will also need shorts for the Egyptian Guards' hats and rags or shredded plastic garbage bags for the Prisoners. Finally, you will need some long streamers tied to short sticks (similar to the ribbons rhythmic gymnasts wave).

Preparation: Place a large chair CS. This will serve as Pharaoh's throne, the altar on which Isaac is nearly sacrificed, the Tower of Babel, and any other structure you may need. If your facility has no offstage wings, use large, flat screens SL and SR for characters to exit and hide behind. Ideally, the projector at the back of the hall should be an old movie projector because it makes that characteristic clicking sound. However, if you can't get one, simply direct a strong flashlight or floodlight at the stage, and have the Projectionist wiggle his or her fingers in front of it to create the flickering effect of a silent movie.

Cue
Stage directions for exits and entrances can be changed depending on the facilities. The ones given here are for a stage that relies mainly on an offstage wing to SL and a small screen to SR. If your stage has heaps of exits, move people around as you please.

Cast of Characters

Dr. Archetype (wears a formal suit or khaki explorer outfit)

Adam (initially wears a sheet then a fig leaf made of green paper)

Eve (ditto, and fig leaves can be ridiculously big)

Cain (wears a semi-caveman outfit made of fur or some such)

Abel (ditto)

Four Angels (wear white sheets with wire-frame paper wings; one carries a sword)

Moth (carries a large cutout of a moth)

Dust Specs (three or so carrying cutouts of brown blobs)

Static (three or so wearing black leotards and waving streamers on sticks)

Five Number Bearers (each carries a poster with a number on it)

Focus Sign (carries the two-sided "Focus" poster)

Mrs. Potiphar (wears a slinky black dress)

Egyptian Guards (two or three bare-chested males wearing towels around their waists and shorts turned upside down and pulled onto their heads to resemble Egyptian hats)

Prisoners (two or three in miserable rags or well-shredded plastic garbage bags)

Projectionist

The following characters can simply wear biblical-looking outfits made of sheets and tea towels:

Noah

Noah's wife and three sons with their wives

Mob (any number in robes)

Abram/Abraham

Sarai/Sarah

Pharaoh

Isaac

Rebekah

Jacob

Esau

Laban

Joseph (wears a colorful jacket)

Brothers (any number up to eleven)

Potiphar

Because this skit has only one speaking role, it is an excellent introduction to drama for kids who want to put on a show but are too scared to tackle one with a lot of lines to learn.

If you don't have enough people for this cast-of-thousands production, many of the actors can each play several roles.

Script

The Genesis Home Movie

Dr. Archetype: *(Enters with box under one arm.)* Hello. Doctor Archetype here of the British Museum's archaeology section. I've just dropped in to give you some idea of the amazing discovery that's just been made by our Middle Eastern department. Yes, it's truly an astounding discovery, a unique find, a treasure of inestimable value to all areas of historical study with stupendous ramifications for theology and archaeology. I'm sure you'll agree with me that it will rewrite our conceptions of ancient history and of cosmology itself. Look for it in newspapers and on TV because, I can assure you, it will be there. Well, thanks for letting me drop in, and I hope I've been able to interest you in this latest development in this fascinating field of study.

(Looks offstage as if being prompted.)

Dr. Archetype: Oh yes, sorry. I didn't tell you what it is, did I? Well, our Middle Eastern team was recently excavating a small ruin in the northern Tigris and Euphrates basin. Seemed to be some very old remains there in the form of a garden gone wild and some evidence of plowed land with small huts. Well, as we were excavating, we uncovered this! *(Holds box up.)* To the untrained eye, it may look insignificant. It is, in fact, a very ancient box. When we pried it open, the most amazing thing fell out. It was a spool of extremely old home-movie film, dated, ooh, I wouldn't like to say when; probably some thousands of years B.C., but still in quite fair condition due to the airtight seal and the dry atmosphere of the immediate environment.

We immediately took it back to London for preservation, of course, and carefully unrolled it. We ran it through an ancient Babylonian film projector which we'd found in the ruins of the audiovisual section of King Nebuchadnezzar's library, and we found it to be a home movie showing the original events described in the book of Genesis. In effect, it would appear that we have stumbled on one of God's own home movies, lost for thousands of years, and now unrolled for all to see.

Why, the contents are staggering. The original movie footage of Creation, the Flood, the patriarchs—it's all there. Amazing stuff and in remarkable condition.

Now just who filmed it all is a bit hard to know. Whether Father God, proud parent of his new children, wanted to keep a film record for memory's sake, a sort of catalogue of their growing up; or whether one of the archangels, Gabriel or possibly Michael, made the film—we may never know. But there it is. Incredible stuff, eh? Imagine, having one of God's own home movies!

Well, let's have a look at it. You'll notice the modern projector at the rear of the building, which has been specially adapted to show this ancient film. Lights please. *(Lights go out.)* Projectionist, you may start whenever ready.

(Dr. Archetype sits, the projector goes on, Projectionist starts wiggling fingers happily in front of the projector, and the action starts onstage. Because all attention is now on the stage, Dr. Archetype can read his or her part from the front row or a seat offstage.)

Dr. Archetype: Now it's not too bad except at the start, where the footage is a bit blurred, but we'll do the best we can. It's silent, of course, and, like all old films, in fast motion. But nevertheless, it is in color. Now here is the leader tape.

(Number Bearers, carrying signs numbered from five to one, run across the stage, followed by Focus Sign, who stands for a few seconds holding up the blurrily written "Focus" side.)

Dr. Archetype: Can we have it a bit more in focus, please?

(Focus Sign bearer turns sign around onto the clearly written side.)

Dr. Archetype: Right, now let's see. This is the blurred bit. Film has degenerated with age, of course. I'd say it's the Garden of Eden and...yes, that's probably Adam and Eve. Just as well it's blurry, considering their early clothing.

(Adam and Eve enter SL with sheets over their heads, thus creating the blurry effect. They wander around, and Adam begins pointing at four progressively taller things.)

Dr. Archetype: Yes, this is Adam and Eve, and here is Adam naming some of the animals, probably the ant, the dog, the giraffe and...(Insert name of a very tall, locally famous person.)*

(Dust Specs and Static race across stage.)

Dr. Archetype: Yes, there is just a bit of dust and some static there.

(Moth races across stage.)

Dr. Archetype: And there's a moth on the projector lens.

(Adam and Eve fling sheets off.)

Dr. Archetype: Well, now here we are after the Fall.

(Cain and Abel enter SL and join Adam and Eve.)

Dr. Archetype: And here is the proud family, Adam, Eve, Cain, and Abel. Fairly happy home scene there *(family group exits SL)*, and here is the part which I think indicates that the home movie was in fact shot by one of the angels.

(Angels enter SL and begin clowning around, making faces, doing dances, making "rabbit ears" behind each other's heads, and so on.)

Dr. Archetype: Yes, here are some informal joking shots of angels clowning around. I think the one with the sword is probably Gabriel, but I'm not sure who the others are. Now watch the looks on their faces; God is about to find out that they are playing with the camera.

(Angels suddenly glance offstage, leap with obvious shock and fear, and race off SL.)

Dr. Archetype: Yes, there it is, so I think it is safe to say that the angels took the official part of this home movie with God performing and directing.

(Static races across stage. Cain and Abel enter SL.)

Dr. Archetype: Now here are Cain and Abel, and, yes this is the sad story of sibling rivalry and the world's first murder.

(Cain belts Abel over head with huge club, and Abel staggers off SL followed by Cain, who is giggling.)

Dr. Archetype: And to think that Cain thought it was a big secret. No wonder God asked, "Where is your brother?" It was God's angels who probably filmed the whole thing.

(Cain enters dejectedly SL and wanders off SR.)

Dr. Archetype: And there goes Cain off to the lands in the east.

(Mob and Noah enter SL. Mob stages general debauchery with mimed drinking, fighting, and so forth.)

Dr. Archetype: Now, here is the society of the time, very debauched as you can see, and, yes…*(Noah stands out of the crowd)* there's Noah, standing out there as the only good man in the world. And here he is receiving God's warning about the coming flood and his instructions to build the ark.

(Noah makes signs to show that he has heard God's call. He waves on his family from SR, and they all begin feverishly miming the building of the ark. Mob exits SL laughing, then runs on again, begging and pleading as Noah and his family close the ark. Mob gives up and swims off SL; Noah and family float off SR waving and smiling. One may be seasick. Static races across.)

Dr. Archetype: Of course, there is no actual footage of the Flood itself. The camera was probably put away for that episode so it would not be damaged in the wet atmosphere.

(Mob enters again SL and begins building.)

Dr. Archetype: Anyway, Noah and his family got out of the ark, and the next thing we see is the arrogant people of the day attempting to build their tower to reach the heavens and rival God. Yes, they're all going about it very quickly,

but something is about to happen. They're about to be struck.

(The facial expressions of the Mob change as they are struck. General misunderstandings occur, and quarrels break out as they gesticulate and mouth words.)

Dr. Archetype: There they go, being struck with different languages. That'll teach 'em, eh?

So we can see the confusion of languages there, and we can also see the origins of some of our present language families. We can't hear it, of course, but the body language and actions allow us to see various national types.

Italian. *(A couple of Mob members exit from Mob SL gesturing with typical "Italian" movements such as arguing, poking each other in the chest, and slapping foreheads in frustration.)*

French. *(Others emerge SL from Mob and use big hand gestures such as joining the finger and thumb tips of right hand and shaking the hand with a loose wrist to emphasize point being made.)*

English. *(Other members of Mob emerge SL looking very contained and conservative. In their calm detachment, they are obviously disgusted at the excesses of more volatile ethnic groups.)*

(Projector turns off.)

Dr. Archetype: And that is the end of the first spool.

Well, it looks as if God is having endless troubles with his new creation of troublesome humans. He creates, and they de-create. Well, in the next section, he tries to re-establish contact with his creation, this time through one special family, and, are we are ready to roll?

(Projector goes on again.)

Dr. Archetype: Now, here we are in the city of Ur.

(Abram enters SR and is praying.) And here is Abram, the son of one of Noah's descendants.

(Abram hears the call, grabs Sarai from SR, and moves off SL.) He has received God's call to go find the Promised Land, and off he goes to he doesn't know where.

(Angels dance on from SL, clown round and dance off SL again.) Oh yes, there are some more of those silly angels goofing around.

(Pharaoh enters SR with Egyptian Guards and sits on throne. Abram and Sarai enter SL and bow before Pharaoh.)

Dr. Archetype: Here we are now in Egypt in Pharaoh's palace, and Pharaoh is obviously noticing the beauty of Sarai, Abram's wife.

(Pharaoh obviously notices her and looks her up and down. She flirts back a

little, and Abram whispers in her ear. She nods and goes on flirting.)

Dr. Archetype: Abram is saying not to tell them she is his wife so the Egyptians won't kill him to get her.

(Guards suddenly fall ill about the place.)

Dr. Archetype: Yes, there is the sickness which was visited on the Egyptians, and there is God telling Pharaoh what is actually going on and how he is flirting with a married woman—very dishonorable.

(Pharaoh looks up to receive message from God and is obviously horrified. He hauls Abram over and makes obvious movements to indicate his displeasure and that Abram is expelled from the country.)

Dr. Archetype: And there's Abram getting bawled out, and off they go—on the road again.

(Abram and Sarai exit SR; Pharaoh and Guards exit SL. Static.)

Dr. Archetype: The next part is a quick bit of the making of the covenant between Abram and God where Abram promises to serve God, and God changes Abram's name to Abraham and Sarai's name to Sarah.

(Abraham enters SR, talks to God, and nods happily.)

Dr. Archetype: And here he is given the command to circumcise himself and his offspring as a sign of his obedience.

(Abraham registers sudden shock. Shakes head in disbelief. Then with drooping shoulders and air of resignation, picks up ax, sword, or other similar implement and trudges off SR. Static. Moth.)

(Abraham, Sarah, and Isaac enter SR, stand, and pose, smiling.)

Dr. Archetype: Some time later now, and we have Abraham and Sarah with their new son, Isaac, born to them in their old age.

(Abraham and Isaac exit SR. Sarah exits SL. Static.)

Dr. Archetype: And, of course, there is the well-known incident when Abraham is called on to offer Isaac to test his obedience to God but is stopped by God at the last instant.

(Abraham, with sword, and Isaac enter SR. Isaac lies down on the altar. Abraham is about to chop when he is stopped. Obvious relief on face of Isaac. Abraham exits SL. Isaac remains. Rebekah enters SR. Mob enter SL and throw confetti.)

Dr. Archetype: Next picture is the wedding of Isaac and Rebekah, and, of course, there is the family shot.

(Mob exit SL, Jacob and Esau enter SL and stand in family shot with Isaac and Rebekah.)

Dr. Archetype: Here they are with their twin sons, Jacob and Esau, and you can certainly see some of the coming conflict which is seen in the next bit.

(Esau shoots a little arrow across stage and goes to retrieve it. As he passes Jacob, Jacob sticks a foot out and trips him. Parental reaction is obvious. Isaac lifts eyes to sky in exasperation and wags finger at Jacob, but Rebekah pets and comforts Jacob, who makes rude signs at Esau. They all exit SL except Jacob and Rebekah, who exit SR. Static. Moth.)

Dr. Archetype: And, yes, this is what it grew into when Isaac and Rebekah were old.

(Isaac enters SL, very old and blind. Jacob enters SR with Rebekah, who secretively covers him with the sheepskin seat cover or whatever furry thing is being used.)

Dr. Archetype: Yes, there it is, the plot to disguise Jacob as his hairy older brother to get the elder son's blessing by deceit.

(Jacob receives Isaac's blessing. Races off SR. Esau enters SL and goes into rage. Exits SR.)

Dr. Archetype: Well that certainly was an unfortunate incident.

(Jacob enters SR pursued by Esau. They race across stage and exit SL. Enter again SL and race across to SR exit. Both use exaggerated running motions, striking and dodging, and exaggerated facial expressions.)

Dr. Archetype: And that's how it went for a few years, really. Not a very close or friendly relationship between brothers there. But I think that at any time now—

(Jacob races back on SR pursued around and around the stage, this time by Laban. Both exit SL.)

Dr. Archetype: Yes, here is Jacob running away from his uncle Laban, whose flocks and herds he has just ripped off. He certainly was a bit of a con artist. No wonder his name means "the ankle tripper." But he couldn't run all the time, could he?

(Jacob enters SL pursued apparently by no one but furtively looking over his shoulder all the time.)

Dr. Archetype: Yes, here he is being pursued by God as well as everyone else.

(Jacob lies down.)

Dr. Archetype: He is tired and lies down and…any moment now…yes, here is the angel of the Lord.

(One of the Angels enters SL and taps Jacob on the shoulder. They wrestle.)

Dr. Archetype: Jacob wrestles with his visitor, the angel of the Lord, and who wins? *(Angel gives Jacob a tremendous kneeing in the hip.)* There it is, the biggest bruise in the Old Testament. It's all in Genesis.

(Angel exits SL, and Jacob limps around. Esau approaches from SR. There is anxiety from Jacob, but Esau races over and bearhugs him. They are reconciled.)

Dr. Archetype: And it all ends happily after all, and just as well, because I don't think Jacob was in much shape to do any more running.

(Static. Dust. Projector suddenly is turned off. Characters onstage stay exactly where they are but just slump over, bent double.)

Projectionist: Sorry. The bulb's blown. I'll just switch to the spare.

Dr. Archetype: Thank you.

Projectionist: OK. Here we go again.

(Projector is turned on again, and characters stand straight and reanimate.)

Dr. Archetype: Sorry about that. Yes there they are, all happy again.

(Esau exits SR and Joseph, in colorful coat, and Brothers enter SL and pose for family shot. Joseph stands next to Jacob, obviously the favorite, and his Brothers grind their teeth at him.)

Dr. Archetype: Well, here we are again with the happy family shot. This is Jacob with his sons. His favorite son, Joseph, is in the famous coat of many colors. The jealousy of the older brothers toward Daddy's favorite is certainly very evident here.

(Static, Dust, Moth race across, and Joseph exits SR.)

Dr. Archetype: Now the next shot is very significant because we can see what has happened in the interim.

(Family shot again. Jacob depressed. No Joseph. Brothers happy and congratulating each other. Family group exits SL. Joseph and Potiphar enter SR.)

Dr. Archetype: Of course, the next shot we have is of Joseph in Egypt in the slave market, where his brothers sent him. There is the official Potiphar buying him. And here is Mrs. Potiphar.

(She slinks on from SL and immediately drapes herself round Joseph as Potiphar is occupied on other side of stage with business.)

Dr. Archetype: But he didn't reciprocate, and then—

(Mrs. Potiphar mouths her yells and screams.)

Dr. Archetype: She yells and screams; yes, there it is, "Rape, rape, rape!" And here come the guards, and he's off to jail.

(Egyptian Guards race on and seize Joseph. He is dragged off SL. Joseph and Prisoners enter SL and Joseph begins to make "interpreting" type movements as the Prisoners sit, obviously amazed.)

Dr. Archetype: Next shot is of Joseph in prison interpreting the prisoners' dreams, and he is now being brought before Pharaoh to interpret the royal nightmares.

(Guards again enter and seize Joseph. Guards, Joseph, and Prisoners exit SL. Pharaoh enters SR and sits on throne as Joseph is dragged on again by Guards from SL and starts to interpret.)

Dr. Archetype: And that's how he did so well.

(Pharaoh and Guards jump up and down with happiness. Pharaoh drapes robes around Joseph. Pharaoh and Guards exit SR. Joseph struts around stage. Brothers enter SL looking hungry and dejected.)

Dr. Archetype: Now, of course, there is the famine in Israel. Here are the brothers come to Egypt to look for food. Don't they get a shock when Joseph lets them know who he really is!

(Joseph reveals his true identity. Brothers in shock.)

Dr. Archetype: But, fortunately, Joseph is very forgiving toward them.

(Happy reunion, then the Brothers race off SL to get Jacob. They bring him back on SL. Another happy reunion.)

Dr. Archetype: All is forgiven. They race off and get old Jacob who just can't believe it's all true. And there's the happy family reunion with the angels happily filming it all. And that's just about where it finishes.

(Static, Dust, and Moth.)

Dr. Archetype: There's just a little bit of waste film at the end here. Not sure what's on it.

(Angels enter SL again and clown round. Exit SR.)

Dr. Archetype: Oh, yes. I might have known.

(Projector turns off. Dr. Archetype stands to address audience.)

Dr. Archetype: Well, there it is, Genesis on film. Very condensed, of course, but that's home movies for you, and it still does give a good overview of what it is all about. Primarily about God's constant efforts to guide and befriend his people, to get back into contact with a disobedient world. Amazing stuff, too.

Well, I've really got to get on my way, you know. The work of digging is still going on, and you never know what you may find, so I've got to get back to my brushing. We may be on the verge of some stupendous new discovery—the home-movie version of Exodus or Samuel. There may be two Samuel movies, you know, Samuel One and Samuel Two. Same as Kings. They'd be fairly violent movies, so I suppose we'd probably have to slap an R rating on them. 'Bye now.

(Exit any side and Curtain.)

The David Mess

Themes: The life of David, God's use of human failure, God's patience

Summary: This skit portrays the life of David, but in its telling, which is full of mistakes and miscues, it makes the point that God uses people to glorify him in spite of their flaws.

Scripture Links: Psalm 71:20; Psalm 103; Luke 15; Ephesians 3:17b-19

Discussion Ideas: This is a very silly skit, but it's hilarious and great fun because it allows the players to legitimately make a whole stack of mistakes that are normally forbidden on stage. Even so, the point it makes is serious. God *does* work with humans even though we *do* make mistakes. God remains faithful to us and continues to work out his purpose through us. The story of David and his career of ups and downs shows how this "man after God's own heart" made errors and fell from grace, as we all do, and yet knew the meaning of repentance and was still a major player in the works of God.

Props and Costumes: You'll need a lectern; an offstage microphone; assorted, mismatched, and anachronistic weapons such as ancient swords, "Stone Age" clubs, baseball bats, and slingshots; armor and uniforms for the armies of the Philistines and the Israelites (these may be made of aluminum foil, which is good because it usually falls to bits as the play proceeds); David's sling (a bit of rope or a leather belt) and a few pebbles; a sword; a broken sword; an earthen pot; two flasks; a cloak; and a club.

Preparation: If your stage is not equipped with substantial wing areas, you will need to place large screens on far SL and far SR because there are a lot of exits and entries in this skit. Other large screens CSR and CSL will conceal various characters and allow numerous mishaps written into the skit. You will also need some sort of screened area USC for Props Person to hide behind. Narrator's lectern is DSR. Post David's lines here and there about the stage as indicated in the script. Suitable areas for "concealing" David's lines will vary with individual stages, but the more unlikely and obvious they are, the better. Post some upside down or sideways so that David has to contort himself to read them. This will increase the comedic effect.

Bike helmets make good armor helmets, as do aluminum mixing bowls. The bowls have the added advantage of looking ridiculous.

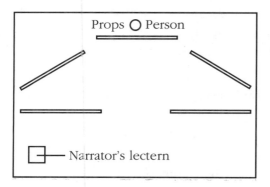

Cast of Characters

Narrator (formal attire and manner)

Props Person (small in stature and fiery)

Samuel (dressed in the robes of a prophet)

Director (becomes more and more frustrated and embarrassed as the mess worsens; formally dressed)

God (offstage voice)

Mob (any number of people to play Jesse's sons, Philistines, and Israelites; dressed in robes, tea towels, sheets, and so on to resemble biblical attire)

Jesse (tends to get carried away; dressed in biblical robes)

Goliath (very dense; heavily armored and armed—positively dripping with weapons)

David (hasn't learned lines at all; dressed in biblical robe or country-boy tunic)

Saul (dressed in kingly robe or armor; wears a crown)

Offstage Voice 1

Offstage Voice 2

Lone Offstage Voice (always calling people in offstage area to be quiet, but no one takes any notice)

Bathsheba (attractive; dressed in biblical clothes that reflect her character)

General (dressed in military dress or armor)

Nathan (frustrated prophet who has good lines but is always being interrupted; dressed in biblical robe)

This skit contains many of the errors that occur on stage in church and Sunday school productions. While making the theological point that God patiently works his purpose through flawed human agents, it will also be very amusing to anyone who has ever tried to stage one of these events. Before the skit begins, have the Director come on stage and say, apparently in all seriousness, that this is the group's first attempt at drama and that the actors haven't had much chance to rehearse. The Director should then sit in the front row of the audience or in some other obvious place to prompt and coach the players.

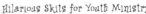

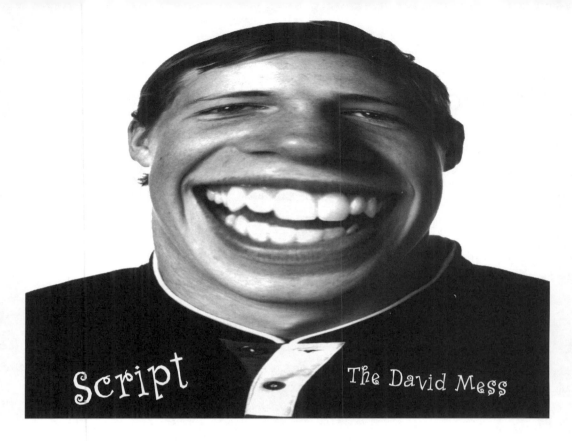

Script

The David Mess

(Narrator enters imperiously and takes up position DSR but effect is ruined when the Props Person tiptoes out and hides behind the screen USC as Narrator is about to commence reading.)

Narrator: Ahem. The story of David. King Saul, first King of Israel, had failed God and been fired. God had rejected Saul as king. God called Samuel, the prophet.

Samuel: *(Enters SR.)* Yes, I shall seek out—

Director: *(Coaching)* Shhhhh!

God: *(The God voice is offstage and is preceded by the entirely audible click of an offstage microphone being clumsily turned on. Lines are delivered mechanically, as if being badly read.)* Seek out the man I have chosen. Go to the family of Jesse, and I will point out to you the man. *(Heavy click.)*

Samuel: *(Has been obviously waiting for his line.)* Yes, I shall seek out this man, Lord. I will go forth.

(Begins to exit SR and suddenly recalls he is supposed to go to SL. Does so apologetically when Director stands and points him off in the correct direction. Moves to SL and speaks into wings.)

Samuel: Jesse, call your sons.

(Jesse steps clumsily and uncertainly on stage from SL.)

Narrator: Jesse called his sons.

Jesse: Sons!

(Fully armed Mob races on from SL and is sent off SL by Director. They leave giggling as they realize that they are not supposed to be on stage yet as the army. They are heard dropping their weapons noisily, and Lone Offstage Voice calls for quiet offstage. Mob offstage responds by loudly hissing, "Shhhhh!" like a lot of steam trains.)

Jesse: Here are my sons, all brave men.

(He indicates behind him and then turns to see there is actually no one there. Nonplused, he looks toward Director.)

Director: *(Stage whisper)* They're coming. Improvise.

Jesse: *(Sudden brilliant flash)* They are not here. They are out in the fields at work…*(warming to the subject)* pouring out their honest sweat, laboring beneath the burning sun of Africa—

(Mob come racing on again SL along with Goliath and David, and all stand happily in line behind Jesse.)

Jesse: *(Pulled up in the middle of his rave, he starts again, somewhat deflated.)* They are all here, all brave men.

Goliath: *(Very dense)* I am Goliath, the great and mighty.

Director: Not yet; get off!

(Goliath deflates and apologetically exits SL.)

Narrator: But God said…

God: *(Offstage, preceded by the usual hefty microphone click)* Seek out the man I have…hold on *(paper rustling as the right line is found)*. None of these is my choice.

Samuel: *(To Jesse)* Are these *all* your sons?

Jesse: No, there is still David, the youngest one. He is not here.

(David suddenly realizes that he isn't supposed to be on stage and tiptoes off SR.)

Samuel: Fetch him for me, Jesse. None of these is God's choice.

(Mob now stampedes off with much laughter and whispering. A couple of Mob members are at the tail end, not really involved with what is going on but leisurely chatting to each other, wandering in and out at the tail end of the rest of the enthusiastic members. When Mob is all offstage, another gale of excited laughter and talking comes from the offstage area. The Lone Offstage Voice calls for everyone to keep quiet. Noise offstage subsides amid hushed giggling. Jesse goes to SR and fetches David, bringing him back to Samuel.)

Narrator: When David came, Samuel knew that this was the right man. God said…

God: *(Offstage with click)* This is the right man. *(Click off.)*

David: *(Obviously reading lines written on his right hand.)* I am the right man.

Narrator: Reaching for a flask of oil, Samuel anointed David.

(Samuel attempts to inconspicuously reach over to the screen USC for the flask the Props Person has for him. Props Person's hand comes out with successively a sword, a pot, a cloak, and finally a flask.)

Samuel: *(Anointing)* I anoint you King of Egypt.

Director: Israel.

Samuel: I anoint you Israel of Egypt.

(Samuel, David, and Jesse exit SL.)

Narrator: And so David was, one day, to be king. But there were mighty deeds for him to do yet. The old enemies of Israel, the Philistines, were on the warpath. King Saul and his army went out to meet them.

(Mob, Saul, and Goliath enter noisily with Mob making savage war cries. They divide into Israelites with Saul on SR and Philistines with Goliath on SL. There is a lot of to-ing and fro-ing as members get confused about which side they are supposed to be on. Goliath is particularly confused and has to be taken across to the Philistines.)

Goliath: *(Standing forward from Philistines)* What? Do they send a boy against me—

Narrator: *(Coaching him)* No, no. I am Goliath.

Goliath: You're not; you're the Narrator.

Narrator: *(Exasperated)* No, it's your line: I am Goliath…

Goliath: Oh, yeah. *(Very mechanically)* I am Goliath, the great and mighty. Send forth a champagne to do battle with me.

Director: Champion.

Goliath: Eh? Oh. Send forth a champion to do battle with me.

Narrator: But David said…

David: *(Enters, trips, stands up again, and sidles across to screen USC as he reads more lines obviously written on the palm of his left hand).* I will fight this giant. *(David is now obviously at the limit of the lines on his palms and from now on will have to read them in various clandestine spots where he has posted them around the stage. He reads now some notes pinned to the side of the USC screen.)*

David: I am not, um…*(pauses to lift page pinned to USC screen)* afraid.

Goliath: *(Pleased that he can at last say his line)* What? Do they send a boy against me? Foolish boy. The bones shall eat your dogs.

Narrator: He picked up his sling.

(Goliath, somewhat puzzled, goes to pick up a sling.)

Narrator: No, David picked up his sling and some stones.

(There is more confusion at the Props Person's USC screen as the wrong things are passed out then swapped for the sling and stones.)

Narrator: And David ran toward the giant.

(David runs right up to Goliath so the two are virtually nose to nose.)

Narrator: When he was still some distance away…*(David, embarrassed, is forced to back away again.)*…he swung his sling and slung a slong…I mean slung a stone. *(David slings.)* It hit Goliath in the head, and the giant fell dead.

Goliath: *(Whispers to Director.)* Now?

Director: *(Exasperated)* Yes, yes.

(Goliath goes into a long, drawn-out dying sequence which he has obviously been looking forward to. It takes him, groaning, arching, bending, choking, throat-clutching all around the stage, right up to the SL end of the Props Person's USC screen, from which point he falls full length, very heavily down behind the Props Person's screen. There is a scream and a terrible crunching crash. Props Person leaps out from behind screen in a rage.)

Props Person: My props! He smashed all my props! *(Holds up a broken sword)* Look at this sword! It took me a week to paint it! *(Goliath quickly stands up and is terribly apologetic as he tries to put things together again, but Props Person is livid. Despite Director's calls for quiet, Props Person heads for Goliath.)*

Props Person: I'll get you for this. Come on, outside right now. Just you and me.

(Despite size and costume, Goliath is obviously terrified by this. It is all the funnier if Props Person is very small in stature. Director finally convinces Props Person to get back behind screen and gets the play going again. Goliath, somewhat shaken by it all, moves aside a little and dies again, lying down quietly and tastefully.)

Narrator: The Philistines were terrified and ran away.

(With a terrible scream, Philistine section of the Mob and Goliath all race off SL.)

Narrator: Now that Goliath was dead—

(Goliath quietly returns to SL. He is standing next to USC screen signaling to Director, asking if this is the right place to die, when Props Person whips out

from behind screen and belts him over the head with a prop club. Goliath goes down with a thud.)

Narrator: Now that Goliath was dead, David was a hero, but Saul was jealous.

Saul: Get me my long sword, and I will kill David.

(Saul reaches out to Props Person's screen and is passed the broken stub of a sword. Nonplused, Saul looks at it as if wondering whether to continue. Props Person peeps out from behind screen.)

Props Person: *(To Saul, indicating Goliath)* He did this.

(Director waves them on, and Saul and David stage a stylized chase around the stage. Israelite section of Mob, which is still on stage, provides enthusiastic applause and encouragement as at a race.)

Narrator: Year after year Saul pursued David, but never did he catch him.

(David trips over something, and Saul falls right on top of him. They assist each other to stand and renew the stylized chase.)

Narrator: At last, the Philistines attacked again, and Saul died on the bottle…sorry, on the battle…*(turning page)* field.

(Philistine section of the Mob races in again, tailing the usual two lethargic Mob members, who are still chatting leisurely, scarcely aware of all that is happening. The Mob race across from SL, trample David, pummel Saul, and race out again over the top of David, who is just getting back to his feet. Again, huge gales of giggling and excited talk are heard as the Mob disappears offstage as the same Lone Offstage Voice yells for silence.)

Narrator: And David became king.

(Israelite members of Mob surround David, smiling hugely and slapping him too heavily on the back.)

Cue

The sound of an explosion can be nicely replicated by standing fairly close to a microphone and puffing into it, but it doesn't do the microphone a whole lot of good if it is too loud and strong. Check with the sound person that you don't have a delicate, sensitive microphone that will be destroyed by this. Alternatively, you may use a taped sound effect of an explosion and play it over the PA system, but be sure to rehearse this with the sound person first to get the timing right.

Narrator: There was clapping and cheering.

(Weak cheers begin from Israelite Mob members but die again as they look around uncertainly, waiting for the sound effects which haven't come.)

Narrator: *(Looking toward sound effects area off SL.)* And there was clapping and cheering.

(There is the sound of an explosion offstage.)

Offstage Voice 1: Sorry. The tape player just blew up.

(In final stages of exasperation, Director races off SL and drags Philistine section of Mob onto SL.

With exaggerated motions, Director conducts a cheer and then pushes them all off again SL. The usual sounds of laughter and the calls for quiet occur again. Director takes seat again.)

Narrator: *(Also exasperated after the drama, in which he or she was to have played so dignified and prominent a role, has been messed up so badly)* After the cheering and clapping, there was much fighting, and David won many victories against his enemies. *(Israelite members of Mob draw swords and hold them high as they march off dramatically SL.)* Then one day, David fell in love with the beautiful Bathsheba, wife of Uriah the Hittite.

(Bathsheba enters SR, and David notices her in a tremendously exaggerated way. He sidles up to her, and they flirt a bit.)

Offstage Voice 1: *(Confidentially)* He really does like her, you know.

Offstage Voice 2: Yeah, she likes him too; look at the way she's—

Offstage Voice 1: Hey, be quiet; the microphone's on.

Offstage Voice 2: Shh. *(The click of a microphone is heard, and the couple stop flirting, obviously embarrassed by this unexpected piece of publicity. Bathsheba exits SL behind the large screen.)*

Narrator: So David said…

David: *(Draws his sword and holds it horizontally in front of his eyes in order to read the notes written along its blade.)* She is beautiful. I must kill her…*(turns sword over to read rest of line)* husband. *(Calls.)* General!

(General enters SR and salutes. David focuses on palm of General's hand, which is held up in salute, and obviously reads the notes he has written there.)

David: *(Mechanically again)* Next time you are in battle, take Uriah and put him in the most dangerous spot where he will be kicked… *(reads closer)* killed.

(General exits SL behind large screen.)

Narrator: And so the deed was done. But Nathan the prophet heard about it, and he came to David and said…

Nathan: *(Entering fearsomely from SR)* You have done evil! You have committed sin in the eyes of the Lord. *(Dramatically, in true Bible-movie-spectacular prophet mode)* The wrath of heaven will now fall on your head—

(At this point, right in the middle of Nathan's rave, the large screen SL, in front of which Nathan and David are standing, collapses on top of Nathan and David. They crumble beneath it with a horrible shriek, as the General and Bathsheba are revealed to be involved in a big, slurpy kiss. Nathan and David crawl out from under the screen. The General and Bathsheba realize that they are out in the open, immediately break the embrace, and pick up the screen. David is now fully distracted by what had been going on behind the screen.)

Nathan: *(Although he tries to get his prophetic rave going again, he has to keep dragging David back to attention as David keeps sidling off to peep around the screen to see what is going on behind it.)* The wrath of heaven—Hey, are you listening?—The wrath of...hey...the wrath of heaven will—

(Finally the Director stomps onto stage, goes behind large screen SL, drags the General out and across stage, and dumps him behind the other large screen SR. For some unknown reason, Goliath enters SL amid the chaos.)

Goliath: I am Goliath, the great and mighty.

Props Person: *(Leaping from behind screen)* I'll get you—

(They tussle, and the Director breaks it up and sends them in different directions. Director resumes seat.)

Nathan: *(Finishing his rave at last)* The wrath of heaven will now fall on your head, OK? *(Stomps off SL. David is left behind, pulling rude faces, blowing raspberries, and making rude signs after him.)*

Narrator: But God forgave David because of his deep remorse...

(David hears the words and immediately stops the raspberries and assumes a deeply remorseful attitude.)

Narrator: ...and faithfulness. *(Almost without caring because the drama has gone so badly)* Despite his shortcomings, he went on to win many victories. This shows how the Lord's plan and purpose can work through people *(loudly directed at David and the stage in general),* even when those people mess everything up—a lot!

(Instantly, terribly loud music blasts out of the sound system. Mob run on and bow frantically, except the lethargic pair at the back who still haven't figured out that this isn't a rehearsal.)

Goliath: *(Enters grandly)* I am Goliath, the great and mighty.

(Props Person races on, seizes Goliath round the throat, and begins to throttle him. The screen SL falls on top of everyone. The Director raises the screen, and with much noise and frustration and people wanting to keep bowing, Director pushes them all offstage. The music suddenly cuts without any fade out. There is a giant outburst of giggling and noise offstage, the Lone Offstage Voice calls for quiet again, and everything is followed by a general shhhh. Only the Director is now left on stage.)

Director: *(Facing the audience with an exceedingly embarrassed smile)* I'd like to thank all those who had any part in this production, and I'd like to inform the Elders Council *(or whoever is appropriate to the local situation)* that I will tender my resignation letter tomorrow.

(Director sidles offstage, and there is a blackout.)

The Fig Tree

Themes: Fruits of the Spirit, Christian ethics and behavior, consistency, hypocrisy

Summary: This is a conversation between a thornbush that claims to be a fig tree and a Jogger who is convinced that it is, in fact, a thornbush.

Scripture Links: Jeremiah 17:10; Luke 6:43-45; 8:15; John 15:4-8; 1 Corinthians 13:1-3

Discussion Ideas: One of the beauties of comedy is that it can be used to present well-known Bible stories and lessons in a new and interesting way. Link this little skit to a reading of Luke 6:43-45, then discuss the fruits of the Spirit, Christian ethics and behavior, or the influence of ideas and beliefs on actions. Delve into the idea that a person's Christian faith should be obvious to others, the dangers of judging by appearances, and the corresponding dangers of acting and appearing in a certain way and yet not expecting to be judged according to those very acts and appearances.

With older kids, discuss relativism and what makes a Christian. The idea that "anyone can be a Christian as long as he or she is sincere" is propounded every day. This little skit deals in a no-nonsense way with the topic of living the Christian life. Use it to roundly and soundly expose the wishy-washy, smoke screen nature of false definitions of "Christian."

Props and Costumes: No props. If you are really keen, you could create a "tree costume" by having the Thornbush hold up some leaves and a big pointy spike, but this isn't vital. The Jogger wears ordinary clothes.

Preparation: Learn the lines. Nothing is needed on stage except the actors. That's what makes this skit a little gem. It's a piece of cake to stage, yet funny and effective.

Cast of Characters

Thornbush

Jogger

The skit could also be linked to the "Dr. Paul" skit (p. 45), which deals with heresies and false prophets in the early church.

Script

The Fig Tree

Scene: *Thornbush stands DSC, singing to itself. Jogger enters any side, wandering along.*

Thornbush: *(Singing)* Oh, I'm a happy fig tree, that's what I am, yeah, just figgin' along, singin' a song, a fig tree, yeah. *(Sees person.)* Good morning.

Jogger: Morning.

Thornbush: You like figs?

Jogger: Eh?

Thornbush: Do you like figs?

Jogger: Oh. Sure. Love 'em.

Thornbush: Like one?

Jogger: *(Puzzled)* Pardon?

Thornbush: *(Insistent)* Do you want a fig?

Jogger: Well, yes. Have you got one?

Thornbush: Course. I'm a fig tree.

Jogger: What?

Thornbush: I grow figs. That's my job. Try one.

Jogger: But you aren't a fig tree.

Thornbush: Yes, I am!

Jogger: No, you're not. You're a thornbush.

Thornbush: Rubbish!

Jogger: You are!

Thornbush: I'm a fig tree!

Jogger: But you haven't got any figs!

Thornbush: Yes, I have.

Jogger: *(Demanding evidence)* Where?

Thornbush: *(Hesitates.)* Um....There.

Jogger: *(Scornful)* That's not a fig; it's a thorn.

Thornbush: Might not be.

Jogger: It is! Look, it's long and spiky. I know a thorn when I see one.

Thornbush: *(Hopefully)* Might be a long, spiky fig.

Jogger: *(Incredulous)* What?

Thornbush: No, no. It might be. There are different types of figs, you know.

Jogger: Yeah, but there are no long, spiky ones.

Thornbush: *(Has a sudden idea.)* Are so! This is an Assyrian fig. They were spiky people, and they liked their figs sharp!

Jogger: Oh, come on!

Thornbush: *(Warming to the topic)* How do you know? Are you some sort of expert? Are you? Are you a fig farmer, a figgyculturalist?

Jogger: Er...No.

Thornbush: *(Conclusively)* Well, there you are! You go making these generalized statements dictating to me what I am.

Jogger: *(Desperately)* But you're a thornbush! I can tell.

Thornbush: Look. What gives you the right to classify me as one thing or another? What makes a fig, anyway? Who says it's got to conform to your narrow, subjective definition?

Jogger: But everybody—

Thornbush: No, not everybody. It's relative, isn't it? To me, I am a fig tree. Just because you want to classify me as something else, that doesn't mean I have to be molded to fit your middle-class, middle-aged mores.

Jogger: But you don't grow figs. You aren't big enough. Fig trees are huge, and you're...well...

Thornbush: *(Indignant)* Yes. Go on. Say it.

Jogger: You're short.

Thornbush: *(With a "You haven't thought of this one, have you?" type of attitude)* What about baby figs? They're short, aren't they? What if I'm a baby fig?

Jogger: *(Conclusively)* Then you wouldn't have figs. Baby trees don't bear.

Thornbush: *(Undefeated)* Well, I might be an advanced one. I might be precocious. I might be an early bloomer. I might have had all bigger brothers and sisters and that made me mature more quickly. See? You don't think of any of these things, do you?

Jogger: But...

Thornbush: *(Plowing on)* You don't take my past history or family background into account. I mean, *(dramatically)* how do you know I didn't go through some terrible trauma which makes me look and act like a thornbush, while underneath I'm really a Freudian fig tree?

Jogger: *(Patiently, with gritted teeth)* Well, did you?

Thornbush: *(With hurt feelings)* As a matter of fact, I did! When I was just a little seedling, in the formative years, I was badly sprayed by a porcupine. *(Tearfully)* And ever since I've been obsessed with prickles! It makes me come out in spikes. It stunts my growth. It makes my figs pointy. And heartless people like you judge me on external appearances!

Jogger: *(Intelligence insulted)* Oh, brother!

Thornbush: *(Melodramatically thumping chest)* In here a little fig tree lies imprisoned!

Jogger: *(Unable to take anymore)* Oh, stop it!

Thornbush: *(Annoyed)* I will not stop it! The least you can do is try one of my figs. Oh, taste and see, for the fig is good.

Jogger: This is a con job. Look. You look like a thornbush. You have leaves like a thornbush. You show me a spike big enough to jab a rhino's backside, and then you try and tell me you're a fig tree.

Thornbush: You're ignoring half the facts!

Jogger: What facts?

Thornbush: I happen to be an advanced, juvenile Assyrian Throng, and if you'd only try eating one of my fruits, you'd see what I mean!

Jogger: Look. Your fruit betrays you. Why don't you face the facts? You're a thornbush.

Thornbush: *(Still hopeful)* Might not be. Might be a daisy.

Jogger: *(Giving up in disgust and exiting)* Oh, this is ridiculous. I'm leaving!

Thornbush: *(Calling after)* Wait! I might be a rare example of the Lesser Lebanese Prickle Daisy, a gorgeous flower with exquisite perfume which...

(Blackout.)

Feeding the Five Thousand and Other Miracles

Themes: Miracles, human attempts to manipulate God, preconceptions about Jesus, God's sovereignty, messianic expectations both in the time of Jesus and now

Summary: This skit is set in the first-century office of Holyland National Promotions, an opportunistic company that makes money promoting big names. Having already handled Moses and Elijah, the company is in a bit of a slump and is looking for a new celebrity. Could Jesus be the one? Will he fit into their plans for him?

Scripture Links: Matthew 16:1-4; 21:23-27; Mark 1:15-18; 8:27-30; Luke 18:31-34

Discussion Ideas: This drama deals with the concept of miracles, of the God who works them in our human sphere, and with the tendency of some people to want to manipulate both God and his miracles. It deals with several well-known miracles of the Old and New Testaments, especially those associated with Moses, Elijah, and Jesus.

A study of the Red Sea crossing, the fire from heaven before the prophets of Baal, the Transfiguration, or any of the miracles of Jesus can lead into a discussion of how some people would have loved to have made Jesus into their ideas of an earthly king. Discuss the messianic expectations of the first-century Judeans and emphasize the ways that Jesus consistently refused to meet them.

And let's not forget that we today can be as tempted to try to manipulate God as anyone in the past. But God is not a "tame" God. He doesn't wait for our cues. He comes and goes as he pleases, regardless of our little designs. This concept can lead to discussions about the unlikely circumstances surrounding Jesus' birth, the paradox of God's choice to be "weak and helpless" in his own creation, and the unusual variety of personality types among the disciples. Kids could also discuss the human tendency to chase and depend on miracles and big, glitzy shows of God's power.

Props: A large "rock" for a child to sit next to (could be a chair covered with burlap or a rough blanket); a newspaper; several chairs, tables, and telephones for an office setting; a map or chart; miscellaneous gear for a musical rock group, such as wires, speakers, and instruments (none of which need to actually work); miscellaneous covered trays, bowls, and so forth for a group of caterers; mops, brooms, and buckets for a group of cleaning people.

Preparation: Divide the stage into two halves, the left and right sides. Set SR as an office scene, with three or four tables, chairs, and telephones. This half of the stage will be used during the first half of the skit. Place the "rock" SL; this will be the scene for the second half of the skit. Thus the skit can flow from one scene to the next without the need for a curtain or blackout. Set up a microphone offstage.

A blackout is a good, quick way to give the Child time to hide next to the rock and for the audience to adjust to the next scene.

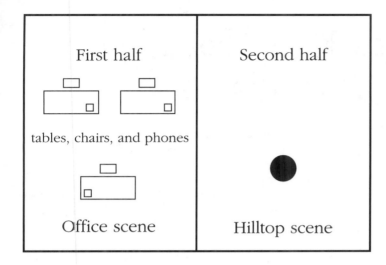

First half

Second half

tables, chairs, and phones

Office scene

Hilltop scene

When Ziggy, of the musical group Ziggy and the Nostrils, is telling his ideas for entertaining in the early part of this skit, improvise additional or alternative dialogue and suggestions for songs, using slightly altered, "biblicised" names of current groups and songs.

Cast of Characters

Promoter 1 (the main driving force)

Promoter 2

Promoter 3

Promoter 4

(Promoters are all dressed for office work. Their clothes range from casual but nice to formal office attire.)

Child (likable; dressed in kid's clothes)

Chef (French; dressed in whites and a paper chef's hat)

Ziggy (offbeat and slightly weird; his attire should suggest this)

Martha (dressed in an apron; her hair is tied up in a scarf)

Nonspeaking roles (all dressed in attire reflecting their trades):

    Assorted Band Members and Roadies

    Assorted Chefs

    Assorted Cleaning People

Script — Feeding the Five Thousand and Other Miracles

Scene: *The office of Holyland National Promotions. Three of the Promoters are leaning over one of the desks looking dismally at some papers which would seem to presage bad news for their company's future. The other is on a phone.*

Promoter 2: Hello, Holyland National Promotions. Yes, sir, we do that sort of work. Well, we basically manage celebrities and events. We provide publicity, backing, catering, advertisements; we book venues; we arrange gigs—all for a very immodest fee. Yes, sir, we can do anything necessary to get you more airplay. What sort of act do you do? Choir of singing camels, eh? Do you sing also? And is it you or the camels who dance? Hold the line please.

(To the other three)

Hey, do we need an animal act?

Promoter 1: *(Without looking up)* Animal act? What do you mean, "animal act"? Every day this office *is* an animal act.

Promoter 3: *(To Promoter 2)* What sort?

Promoter 2: Fourteen camels. Sing, dance, and juggle.

Promoter 4: Juggle?

Promoter 2: They roll their backs up and down.

Promoter 1: *(Throwing hands in air)* Singing camels? Backs rolling up and down? If I want to see that, I can look at a graph of the national economy. No way. Get rid of him. Nooo way!

Promoter 2: *(Back on the phone)* Are you there? Look, it sounds great, fantastic. We'd love to promote this act. It's really going to make it. But we feel you may need a little more experience first, so we suggest you play a few shows in…um…

Promoter 1: *(From the background)* Rome.

Promoter 2: *(On the phone)* Rome.

Promoter 3: *(From the background)* In the Coliseum.

Promoter 2: In the Coliseum. They have great animal acts there—elephants, camels, *(quietly)* lions…Yep, right, bye-bye. *(Hangs up.)* Enjoy the lions.

Promoter 4: Hope the lions enjoy you.

Promoter 1: *(Pacing up and down)* Why, why, why? Camels that sing and juggle! How are we supposed to build a promotion company on this sort of stuff?

Promoter 2: We've had nothing for centuries. Nothing worth anything.

Promoter 3: *(Hopefully)* We had an offer yesterday.

Promoter 4: Yeah? From whom?

Promoter 3: *(Trying to help)* Judas the Star Swinger.

Promoter 4: Judas the Star Swinger! What is he—an astronaut turned trapeze artist?

Promoter 2: Some hillbilly hermit who thinks he's God.

Promoter 1: And he wants us to promote him. Book venues, cater, set up posters and ads. Ha!

Promoter 3: *(Still the optimist)* He's got a great speaking voice.

Promoter 1: He'll need it—to give excuses to the Romans when they hang him.

Promoter 2: What about John the Baptist? He was a chance. We offered him a good package.

Promoter 1: And where did it get us, eh? Eh? We had a great image worked out for him.

Promoter 2: Expensive clothes. Sophisticated atmosphere.

Promoter 3: First class food laid on free for his followers, riverside buffet format.

Promoter 4: We could have really taken him places.

Promoter 1: So what does he do?

Promoter 2: Camel's hair clothes.

Promoter 3: Old Testament prophet image—it's all been done before.

Promoter 1: Locust and honey sandwiches.

Promoter 2: And he had the drawing power, good crowds.

Promoter 4: And where did he end up?

(All three do a neck-slicing movement and grimace.)

Promoter 1: Call that a career worth promoting? What we need is someone who's on his way up.

Promoter 2: Someone we can create an image for, promote, manage his appearances.

Promoter 3: Watch him soar and explode in a shower of fame and fortune.

Promoter 1: And money!

Promoter 2: Money!

Promoter 3: Money!

Promoter 4: Especially money!

(Pause.)

Promoter 2: There's King Herod.

Promoter 1: Herod! Ha! He's so busy looking through the latest fashion magazines he's hardly got time to adjust his lipstick.

Promoter 4: *(Horrified)* Shh. Someone will hear you.

Promoter 1: Who cares? We're all washed up. We haven't seen a decent talent since Moses gave that giant pool party by the Red Sea.

Promoter 2: Now that was an event worth promoting. Wow. Waters parting! We had publicity material in every Egyptian army post in the area.

Promoter 3: Boy, they came by the thousands.

Promoter 1: Right into the Red Sea.

Promoter 2: And we laid on an eighteen-track musical backing. And the waters parted.

Promoter 3: And the army came.

Promoter 4: And the waters joined again.

Promoter 1: Boy, that was a show and a half! Did we ever make cash on that one!

Promoter 2: Yeah, especially out of the used chariots.

Promoter 3: Remember the big posters we made up? *(Remembering)* "Thousands of slightly water-damaged, ex-army chariots at craaazy prices."

All: *(Sing or chant)* Low, low prices, two-year guarantee, red-hot specials, by the Red Sea.

Promoter 1: Those were the good old days.

Promoter 2: We need another Moses. Or an Elijah. He was good value.

Promoter 3: Elijah—now there was a talent. Remember the big barbecue he put on for the prophets of Baal?

Promoter 1: Wow, what a gig that was! We had an audience of four hundred prophets of Baal at that one.

Promoter 4: Fire from heaven. What an effect!

Promoter 3: Lively audience, too. Dancing around, slashing themselves. Very lively.

Promoter 2: Except at the end. They weren't so lively then.

Promoter 1: Who cares? They'd all paid for their tickets.

Promoter 3: We didn't guarantee a safe show.

Promoter 1: Whatever happened to those good old days? Moses, Elijah. They could really put on a show.

Promoter 4: *(Hopelessly)* Who is there now?

Promoter 3: *(Reading from a newspaper he has just picked up)* Jesus of Nazareth?

Promoter 4: *(Clicks fingers.)* Oh, I've heard of him. Isn't he some sort of magician?

Promoter 1: Isn't he the guy who pulls fish out of a hat or something?

Promoter 3: Sort of. He makes them appear in the water so the fishermen can get a decent catch.

Promoter 2: Hmm…a bit ordinary. I suppose it would go over all right with the deep-sea sports types.

Promoter 3: He tells good stories.

Promoter 4: Needs to be more than that. That's kid stuff.

Promoter 3: He turns water into wine.

Promoter 1: *(Waking up)* Hey! That could be something. Free grog! We could set him up in opposition to the Mizpah Microbrewery *(or insert name of locally known brewery)*.

Promoter 3: He heals the sick.

Promoter 4: Now, that's not a bad package. Look—a total service. Come along, listen to stories, get drunk on the free wine, and when you wake up…he'll cure your hangover.

Promoter 1: *(Seeing possibilities)* The man's a mobile feast. He could become very, very popular. Think of the crowds he'd draw!

Promoter 2: He could be worth looking into. We could do big things for him.

Promoter 3: *(They all look over Promoter 3's shoulder at the newspaper.)* Rumor has it that he's coming through this way in the next couple of days and is likely to preach on top of the hill next to Lake Tiberias.

Promoter 1: *(Dives to a map on the desk.)* Hmm…good setting. Lakeside. Hey! We could get him to turn the lake water into wine. A lake of wine! Wow!

Promoter 4: *(Mesmerized)* The shoreline would be worth a fortune. *(Leaping into action)* I'll get onto a real estate agent and see if we can buy up some of that lakeside land.

Promoter 3: This could be big, big, big! We could bill him as "Jesus the Great." No—it needs to be more exotic.

Promoter 1: "Jesus the Unbelievable"?

Promoter 2: Hey, Italian! That will get the Romans in. "Guiseppi the Unbelievable"!

Promoter 3: But that might put the locals off. What about "Jerusalem Guiseppi the Unbelievable"? That sounds heaps better than Jesus of Nazareth.

Promoter 4: I mean, Nazareth—who's heard of it? Nazzzareth. Sounds like a mosquito buzzing.

Promoter 1: Right. Let's promote. We'll set him up as the biggest gig of the decade. When did you say he's due?

Promoter 3: Couple of days. Rumor is that he'll come across the lake and then he usually goes up a hill to preach.

Promoter 1: Right. If he's as popular as you say, there'll be a crowd waiting for him.

Promoter 2: They'll need food. We'll book caterers.

Promoter 3: They'll get bored waiting. We'll book entertainment.

Promoter 4: Cleaning up after the event. We'll book that cleanup mob. *We'll* do the management side of things. Wow—it'll all be there waiting for him. He won't be able to refuse a promotion package like this one.

Promoter 3: Crowd estimates are three or even four thousand.

Promoter 2: Fantastic! We'll take this guy and make him a celebrity, a star, *(mesmerized)* a *god!*

Promoter 1: *(to Promoter 2)* You—get on the phone. Book caterers. Get that French mob who did Solomon's feast the time the Queen of Sheba dropped over.

Promoter 2: Right.

Promoter 1: *(To Promoter 3)* And you—for music get that mob that played the loud heavy metal gig we did a few years back.

Promoter 3: The *really* loud one?

Promoter 1: Yeah. It knocked 'em flat. *(Racking his brains)* Where was that gig?

Promoter 3: Jericho.

Promoter 1: That's it. And for cleanup, I'll ring Martha's Cleaning Service. Get to it. This Jesus guy is going to make us some money.

Promoter 4: I'll start calculating ticket sales now. Let's see…four thousand people at thirty dinars each…

All: Wow!

(Promoter 4 exits, still calculating. The rest dive for their phones.)

Promoter 2: *(On the phone)* Hello. Head chef, please.

(Chef's voice can come from offstage, or Chef can step onto stage from either wing and step off again when conversation is over. This will allow gesticulations and so on.)

Chef: Pierre de Lingerie speaking. What do vous want?

Promoter 2: Hi there, Pierre. Holyland National Promotions here. We were wondering if—

Chef: *(Interrupting)* Excuse me. *(Off phone)* Take all ze fur off zat cat *before* it goes in. *(On phone again)* Oui?

Promoter 2: We were wondering if you could do a cheap version of the buffet you did for Solomon a few years back.

Chef: Ah oui. Ze full-range special. What are you promoting?

Promoter 2: We got a prophet going.

Chef: Ah, we have a lovely one for zat. Prophet parfaits—light creamed fruit jellies wiz a touch of sweet almond grasshopper sauce—very popular since John ze Baptist.

Promoter 2: Fine, fine. We'll mail you the details. Three or four thousand people at…

Chef: And zen, served on a bed of…*(off phone)* Is zat ze rare steak? You 'ave to kill it first.

(Promoter 2 hangs up and scribbles details of the conversation.)

Promoter 3: *(On phone)* Hello, Action Music? I want to speak to Ziggy. Yes, Ziggy, lead singer of Ziggy and the Nostrils.

(Ziggy could also step onto stage and conduct his end of the conversation visible to the audience, as with Pierre.)

Ziggy: 'Ullo. Ziggy 'ere. What can I do for you, man?

Promoter 3: We got a gig geared up for you.

Ziggy: Unreal.

Promoter 3: Hilltop venue. Three to four thousand people. We'll mail you the details

Ziggy: Sounds great, man. What sort of image you want?

Promoter 3: General promotion. Background psych music for a prophet. Entertainment if it doesn't pull off.

Ziggy: Great, man. We can, like, turn it into a mega rave party. Prophet, eh? We could do a classic rock number like, um, I hear it now, a little sax line in there, then do it techno to the end for dancing. How about this? *(Singing)*

"God spoke to me;

He gave me all the news.

I came 'round here to give it to youse,

But don't you step on my blue suede sandals."

Yeah, we can work with that, yeah.

Promoter 3: Fine. We'll send you the specifications.

Ziggy: We'll be there. You know our motto: "Ziggy and the Nostrils. You call—we run."

Promoter 3: 'Bye. *(Hangs up and turns to Promoter 1.)* How's it all going?

Promoter 1: Fine, fine. Only one lot to call. *(Takes a breath for what is obviously going to be an unpleasant job.)* Martha's Cleaning Service.

Promoter 3: *(Realizing the implications and sympathizing)* Right.

Promoter 1: While I'm on that, check our stocks on the exchange. Our prices are about to rise, rise, rise. *(Promoter 3 exits. Promoter 1 advances to phone and dials.)* Hello, is Martha there? I'd like to speak to her, please.

(Martha could also step on stage.)

Martha: *(A loud, bulldog type)* What do you want?

Promoter 1: Hello, Martha, it's…er…me.

Martha: *(Sudden change)* Oh, so it's you.

Promoter 1: Yes, it's me.

Martha: You married yet?

Promoter 1: Er, no.

Martha: Nor am I.

Promoter 1: Oh, how nice. I mean, what a shame.

Martha: So what can I do for you, honeybundle?

Promoter 1: We got a big job for you. Concert. Wide area. Food scraps and containers over several hectares. We need cleaning people who can pull it all off.

Martha: We'll be there. Want me to come 'round to your place tonight and get the details?

Promoter 1: *(Jumping)* No, no, no! We'll mail them. 'Bye. *(Hangs up.)* That woman is like a bulldozer.

Promoter 4 : *(Enters.)* All set. We've got sales contracts on 26,000 hectares of lakeside real estate. Effectively covers this whole side of the lake where the wine should be strongest.

Promoter 1: Great.

Promoter 3: *(Enters.)* I leaked a few bits of info onto the exchange about a future gig.

Promoter 2: Our shares are going to go up, up, up.

Promoter 1: They'll be worth a fortune in a few days. Right, *(to Promoter 2)* you take a fast chariot and get up on that hill next to the lake. Get there a day early and scan the place. If Jesus arrives ahead of time, delay the crowds.

Promoter 2: I'll get the band to distract them.

Promoter 1: Great. We've got to get to this Jesus guy and do a couple hours of makeup and image work on him first. Otherwise he'll mess it up.

Promoter 2: Right.

Promoter 1: Guys, this is going to be big, big, big. This will make Woodstock look like an evening of hymn singing.

Promoter 2: The biggest event since Moses and Elijah.

Promoter 3: This Jesus character will get there and find us ready with a promotion package he can't resist. And it's on from there to fame, reputation, money!

Promoter 4: Who knows? We could play Babylon, Jerusalem, Rome—

All: But not the Coliseum!

(Scene change can be effected with blackout or simple exit of characters. New scene is the hilltop with small Child seated behind the rock SL, but still visible to audience. Promoter 1, Promoter 3, and Promoter 4 enter SR. They don't see Child at first.)

Promoter 1: This is the place. Where's what's-his-name? He's supposed to be waiting for us.

Promoter 3: What a dump. We'll really have to do something with the layout.

Promoter 1: We should have brought in some landscapers. Deathly quiet. Not a soul. What a hole.

Promoter 3: Oh, well. Let's get started. Now, music will need to be inconspicuous.

Promoter 1: We can put the group up there behind that clump of trees and hide their speakers behind rocks like this one. *(Looks behind rock and finds Child.)*

Child: Hello.

Promoter 1: Oh yeah, hi, kid. Look, you'll have to move. We're setting up a big show for Jesus of Nazareth…*(Promoter 4 nudges him.)* I mean for Jerusalem Guiseppi the Unbelievable.

Child: But Jesus has already been here.

Promoter 1: Yeah, sure. Now caterers' wagons will go—*(Sudden realization, turns to Child again.)* What?

Child: He's already been. He was here yesterday.

Promoter 4: Yesterday! We missed him. The rumors must have been a day late.

Promoter 3: Sorry. That's what the newspaper report reckoned.

Child: And he used my lunch.

Promoter 4: Huh?

Child: He used my lunch.

Promoter 4: For what?

Child: To feed all the people. I had five loaves and two fish, and he used them to feed all the people.

(Promoters 1, 3, and 4 are thunderstruck. Mouths agape, they can barely speak.)

Promoter 1: Five loaves and two fish?

Promoter 3: Thank heavens we didn't associate our names with this gig.

Promoter 4: He couldn't have drawn more than twenty people!

Child: There were about five thousand men, plus women and children.

Promoter 4: What?

Promoter 3: He fed eight thousand people with five loaves and two fish? What sort of fish?

Promoter 1: Is your dad's name Jonah?

Child: I don't know how he did it, but we all had heaps to eat, and besides, he used—

Promoter 4: Yeah, yeah, all right. He used your lunch. *(Aside to Promoter 1 and Promoter 3)* Can this kid be for real?

Promoter 3: *(To Child)* Have you been dreaming or running a high fever?

Child: Nope. I've just been sitting here all night thinking about it. You see, he used—

Promoter 1: Yeah, fine, congratulations. *(Turning back to general scene)* Where is what's-his-name?

Promoter 2: *(Enters casually SR.)* Hi, guys.

Promoter 1: Hi, guys? We got thousands of dollars of gear coming for a gig that's already happened, and all you can say is "Hi, guys"?

Promoter 2: Yeah. He was here yesterday. I couldn't get word to you, so I had to just sit and listen. I was pretty worried about it—at first.

Promoter 3: So what sorts of things was he saying?

Promoter 2: Oh, about loving God and your neighbor, sharing with those in need, following him.

Promoter 4: *(Exasperated)* Oh, no! He'll get nowhere with that sort of stuff.

Promoter 3: Sentimental garbage. Nothing radical? Nothing political?

Promoter 2: Oh, it was radical all right. But not political.

Promoter 1: We've got to get to this guy before he ruins his own image.

Promoter 2: Well, you guys go on. I've…er…got a bit of…er…thinking to do.

Promoter 1, 3, and 4: Thinking?

Promoter 2: Yeah. I have to replan a few things.

Promoter 1: Replan! What are you talking about? There's money to be made!

Promoter 2: Yeah, sure. You go on and make it. I'll see you tomorrow. *(Turns to go.)*

Promoter 3: *(Exasperated)* What is this? We got a big gig for this Jesus guy, and you want to miss it?

Promoter 2: *(Turning back before exiting and struggling to explain)* Look, it's not the same anymore. The whole world looks different all of a sudden. OK? There are other things…*(Exits.)*

Promoter 4: *(Calling after Promoter 2)* But listen—

Promoter 1: Leave him, leave him! He's lost touch with reality. *This (gesturing around)* is the reality we face at present!

Promoter 3: What are we going to do? We've got all this stuff coming.

Promoter 1: *(Tense)* I know.

Promoter 4: Cleaners, caterers, musicians. Thousands' worth!

Promoter 1: I know, I know. Just let me think.

(Ziggy bursts onto the scene SL with Band Members, Roadies, gear, wires, speakers, and as much stuff as you can muster.)

Ziggy: Greetings, man. Where's the scene? You mean, like, this is the venue? *(Snaps fingers, claps, listens.)* It's pretty non-acoustic, man. We'll set up some bounce walls there. Speakers can go over…*(He wanders around talking to Band Members who enthusiastically begin to silently set up.)*

Promoter 3: *(To Promoter 1, who has head in hands)* The band. We're paying them ten thousand dollars, plus transport and freight.

Promoter 1: I know.

(Pierre, at the head of a line of Chefs carrying trays and other catering equipment, flounces theatrically onto the scene from SL.)

Chef: 'Ello. We 'ave some refrigeration, I 'ope, or else the prophet parfaits will run. *(Turns to Chefs.)* All right, mes amis, set up the tables there. The cat roast…I mean the lamb roast we can serve over there…*(They silently but busily begin setting up.)*

Promoter 4: Caterers. Twenty-six thousand dollars' worth of food, plus waiters' wages.

Promoter 1: I know.

(Martha, with an army of Cleaning People, marches onto scene, perhaps through the audience. Their mops are over their shoulders military style, and their buckets are at the ready.)

Martha: Halt! All right, this is it—at ease! *(Sidles to Promoter 1.)* Hello, dreamboat. Where's the party? Where's the mess? Do you want a full mop job or just the dry broom and brush?

Promoter 3: Cleaning contract worth over seventeen thousand dollars.

Promoter 1: This can't be happening to me. Someone bring me back to the old days with Moses and Elijah.

Martha: *(To Promoter 3)* What did he say?

Promoter 4: He said this can't be happening.

Martha: Why not?

Promoter 3: The show's off.

(All stop and turn to the speaker.)

All: What??

Promoter 1: *(Standing to face the music like an aristocrat going to the guillotine)* The show's off. Jesus has been and gone. We were misinformed on the timing of the whole gig.

(There is a general uproar as Chefs, Band Members, Cleaning People all yell and gesticulate about how much gear they've had to bring, what's going to happen to it all, and so on. Promoters 1, 3, and 4 confer frantically SR.)

Promoter 1: *(Reaching a decision and turning to crowd.)* Quiet, quiet! There's still a chance we can save the situation. *(To Child)* Kid, this Jesus character. When he fed the crowd—

Child: With my lunch—

Promoter 1: Yeah, yeah, with your lunch, did he or anyone else mention where he was going next?

Child: He said he was going to walk across the lake and then go up a mountain to talk to Moses and Elijah.

(This is a bombshell. Promoters 1, 3, and 4 gape at each other.)

Promoter 1: Moses and Elijah!

Promoter 3: Heyyy! This is just like the good old days.

Promoter 4: Moses, Elijah, and Jesus. A three-star billing. What a concept!

Promoter 3: *(Ecstatic)* What a crowd!

Promoter 1: *(To various groups)* Pierre, load up the parfaits again. Ziggy, we're going to need music—lots of music. And Martha, dear Martha. Allow me to carry that heavy broom.

Martha: Ooh, you charmer.

Promoter 1: You look like a million one-hundred-dollar notes—all wrinkly.

Martha: Ooh, you sweet-talker.

(The various groups happily pack their stuff and prepare to leave.)

Promoter 1: We'll set up that mountaintop. We'll put up shelters.

Promoter 3: *(With a sudden brilliant idea)* Tents! We'll put up three tents. One for Jesus, one for Moses, and one for Elijah.

Promoter 4: And we'll charge people to come and look in the tents.

Promoter 3: And we'll put in sideshows, roller coasters, merry-go-rounds.

Promoter 1: This'll be better than…*(Insert name of local well-known school event or church event.)*

Promoter 3: I can hear it now. Hurry, hurry, hurry. Come and see them—the amazing trio of prophets!

Promoter 4: Ready to grant wishes, foretell the future…

Promoters 1, 3, and 4: …or do anything *you* want them to.

(All exit SL. Curtain.)

Dr. Paul

Themes: Heresies, the true Gospel, staying on the straight and narrow, the human aspect of the early church, Paul's epistles

Summary: Dr. Paul, spiritual physician to the early church, has a busy day as church after church comes into his office for treatment for a plethora of ailments. In the process, the audience learns that the modern church still struggles with many of the problems faced by the early church.

Scripture Links: 1 Corinthians; 2 Corinthians; Galatians; Ephesians; Colossians; Hebrews

Discussion Ideas: This skit is an excellent way to introduce some of the issues and situations addressed by Paul's epistles. With an older audience, this could lead to discussions of the specific teachings of some of the early heresies (Gnosticism, for example) and their parallels to modern movements and cults.

Props: You will need two desks or tables; three chairs; cards and papers; a bedsheet; a briefcase or medical bag; a roll of toilet paper with scribblings on it; and axes, knives, chain saws, or other similar, hefty cutting devices.

Preparation: Set the stage to resemble a doctor's office. Set the Receptionist's desk SL and Paul's desk CS. Set a chair on both sides of Paul's desk. (This desk will also be the bed on which Galatians reclines later in the skit.)

Cue

Many of the lines in this play come virtually from Paul's letters. The references are given in brackets for study and follow-up purposes and are not meant to be spoken by the characters.

Cast of Characters

Voice Over

Paul (no-nonsense type, doesn't mess around with half-measures; dressed in a white coat or surgeon's scrubs)

Receptionist (dressed as a medical receptionist or in nurse's whites)

Ephesians (confused and mixed up; attire should reflect this)

Colossians (apologetic and lacking in confidence; dressed conservatively and slightly dorkish or out of fashion)

Nuisances 1, 2, and 3 (condescending and irritating; wear biblical robes)

Corinthians (a cool guy, full of himself; trendy attire)

Hebrews (speaks in a baby goo-goo voice; wears a giant diaper and sucks on a pacifier)

Galatians (timid male; wears pajamas)

Judaizers 1, 2, and 3 (crawly, annoying fellows; wear biblical robes)

Script
Dr. Paul

Scene: *Dr. Paul's surgery. Receptionist is seated, filing cards and papers.*

Voice Over: Any lines in this play which sound like they have been taken directly from the letters of Paul in the New Testament, probably have been. Enter, Dr. Paul, doctor of apostolic psychiatry, obstetrics, and general spiritual physician to the early church.

(Paul enters SL with briefcase and stops at Receptionist's desk.)

Receptionist: Good morning, Dr. Paul.

Dr. Paul: Morning, Kyrie.

Receptionist: A busy day coming up, doctor. Several patients have booked, and there's that house call.

Dr. Paul: Well, who's on the list today?

Receptionist: *(Checking papers)* Well, there's Ephesians.

Dr. Paul: Ah, yes. A form of a multiple personality disorder, I understand. Actually, I'm not all that familiar with Ephesians—one of the few churches whose birth I didn't assist. For the others, I was obstetrician, you know.

Receptionist: Then there's Colossians.

Dr. Paul: With a rapidly developing inferiority complex.

Receptionist: Then there's Corinthians.

Dr. Paul: Just the opposite. A rapidly developing superiority complex, compounded by delusions of grandeur.

Receptionist: Hebrews.

Dr. Paul: Fixated in the juvenile stage. Can't face adult reality or responsibility.

Receptionist: And finally, there's the house call on Galatians.

Dr. Paul: Ah, yes, a most interesting case of masochistic self-mutilation. Well, should be an active day. Send in Ephesians as soon as he (she) comes in, please.

Receptionist: Yes, doctor.

(Paul crosses to his own desk and unpacks a few papers and things. Is seated and checking notes when the angry voice of Ephesians is heard from offstage.)

Ephesians: Walk, won't you, you stupid feet! No, not that way. Straight ahead. Swing, arms. Go on, swing or we can't walk without unbalancing. *(Ephesians enters SL walking in a very uncoordinated fashion, angrily addressing parts of body.)* Now swing in time with the feet. I don't care if you don't like it. *(Shuts eyes.)* Oh, no! Now my eyes have gone on strike. Open up. I can't see.

Receptionist: Go straight in, please.

Ephesians: *(To feet)* Well, you heard the lady. Walk! *(Gropes his or her way to Paul's desk.)* Doctor, you've got to help us. Where are you? My eyes just went on strike.

Dr. Paul: What on earth is the problem? *(Begins to take notes as Ephesians speaks.)*

Ephesians: Well, we're just not working together. There's a theological difference between the hands and the head, and they keep fighting.

(Hands suddenly hit head, once, twice, and on the third time, teeth catch hands and begin to bite them. Appropriate noises from Ephesians.)

Ephesians: There's a personality clash between feet and eyes, and the eyes won't guide the feet. The ears want to be on top of the head because they think they are the most important. The stomach is in a knot, and the intestines are on strike because they're sick of doing all the dirty work.

(Flops down in chair, exhausted, and keeps wriggling uncomfortably, but not enough to distract the audience from what Paul is saying.)

Dr. Paul: Look, you've got to make every effort to preserve the unity of the spirit through the bond of peace [Ephesians 4:3].

Ephesians: Unity?

Dr. Paul: Each of us has received a special gift in proportion to what Christ has given [4:7]. He appointed some to be apostles, others to be evangelists, prophets, pastors and teachers [4:11]. And so, we all come together to that oneness in our faith and in our knowledge of the Son of God [4:13].

Ephesians: But how does that apply to us? *(Feet try to walk away while Ephesians is still sitting.)* Come back, feet!

Dr. Paul: Under his control all the parts of the body fit together and the whole body is held together by every joint. So when each separate part works as it should, the whole body grows and builds itself up through love [4:16].

Ephesians: But what do we have in common?

Dr. Paul: There is one body and one spirit just as there is one hope to which God has called you. There is one Lord, one faith, one baptism [4:4-5].

Ephesians: Hey, yeah! That's great. I never thought of it like that. *(Looks down shirt front and calls out)* Does that make sense, people? *(Suddenly, whole body is still and then begins to work properly, starting with hands traveling slowly to face and patting head, which kisses them.)* Look, hands and head aren't fighting. *(Eyes open.)* Eyes are guiding feet at last. Ears have stopped burning. Stomach isn't knotted any more. And intestines aren't on strike any—excuse me! *(Rushes off SL.)*

Dr. Paul: That's much healthier.

(Colossians enters apologetically and stands uncertainly at Receptionist's desk.)

Receptionist: Doctor Paul, Colossians is here.

Dr. Paul: Send him (her) in.

(Colossians advances apologetically to Paul's desk.)

Dr. Paul: Come in. Sit down.

Colossians: *(Sitting on edge of chair)* Yes, doctor. Sorry.

Dr. Paul: Sorry? Sorry for what?

Colossians: Oh, I don't know. I probably did something wrong.

Dr. Paul: How've you been?

Colossians: Oh, OK. How's life for you, doctor?

Dr. Paul: Oh, busy.

Colossians: Oh, yes. *(Uncertainly tries a joke)* No rest for the wicked, eh? *(Nervous laugh, which is silenced by an icy stare from Paul.)* Oh, no, I did it again. Sorry. Honestly, I am. Sorry.

Dr. Paul: What are you always apologizing for? There's nothing visibly wrong with you. As a matter of fact, we have heard of your faith in Jesus Christ and your love for all God's people [Colossians 1:3-4].

Colossians: That's just it. I don't feel as if we're really Christians. I mean, not fully, you know?

Dr. Paul: Go on.

Colossians: Well, I keep hearing funny voices from within my congregation.

Dr. Paul: And what do they tell you?

Colossians: Well, they tell me…*(Holds head.)* Oh, no. Here they come again!

(Nuisances 1, 2, and 3 dance on from SR and sing in harmony.)

Nuisances 1, 2, and 3: We're here again!

Nuisance 1: *(Slick sales pitch)* We're here again, and hello, hello, hello. Here we are with our new, improved brand of Christianity.

Nuisances 1, 2, and 3: *(Singing)* A new, improved Christ for youuuuu.

Nuisance 2: Fed up with the old Christianity as presented to you by Paul? Well, we have more.

Nuisances 1, 2, and 3: *(Singing)* More, more, more.

Nuisance 3: There's all the thrill of this extra, new, alluring philosophy.

Nuisance 1: The feeling of superiority from being in contact with not just Jesus, but with angels…

Nuisance 2: …demons…

Nuisance 3: …the elemental forces of nature!

Nuisance 1: And the buzz of being part of the elite group that knows all the secret systems and signs while the rest don't.

Nuisance 2: Your old brand-B Christianity is the out-of-date, obsolete one.

Nuisance 3: With us you can have sooo much more.

Nuisance 1: *(Sudden change from slick sales pitch to a "now the small print" seriousness)* Provided you obey all the rules…

Nuisance 2: …and observe the special days…

Nuisance 3: …weeks…

Nuisance 1: …and months.

Nuisance 2: Here's the list of rules. *(Unrolls long roll of toilet paper with scribbling all over it and passes it to Colossians, who shrinks from it.)*

Nuisance 3: *(Reeking of superiority)* We'll be back later to see if you've made the grade yet.

(Nuisances 1, 2, and 3 exit SR imperiously.)

Colossians: *(To Paul)* So you see, I'm inferior! I haven't got it all yet. *(Breaks into weeping.)*

Dr. Paul: This is ridiculous. I tell you, don't let anyone deceive you with false arguments, no matter how good they seem to be [2:4]. See that no one traps you with the worthless deceit of human wisdom [2:8]. God has brought you to new life with Christ. God forgave us all our sins; he canceled the record of our debts with its binding rules by nailing it to the cross [2:13]. So don't allow yourselves to be condemned by anyone who claims to be superior because of special visions [2:18]. And let no one make rules about what you eat or drink or about holy days or the Sabbath [2:16]. You have died with Christ and are set free from the ruling spirits of the universe [2:20].

Colossians: You mean these guys are talking a lot of—

Dr. Paul: *(Interrupting)* Precisely.

Colossians: Then I don't need any of this extra stuff? *(Indicating the roll of rules.)*

Dr. Paul: Exactly.

Colossians: I've got Christ in my heart. That's all I need.

Dr. Paul: Christ is the visible likeness of the invisible God. Christ existed before all things and in union with him all things have their proper places [1:15-17].

Colossians: That's great. I feel so much more sure of myself. I've got it!

Dr. Paul: Always remember, faith in Christ is able to take you to the heights of spiritual experience. He is the key that opens all the hidden treasures of God's wisdom and knowledge [2:3].

Colossians: Thanks a lot, doctor.

Dr. Paul: You must, of course continue faithful on a firm foundation, and must not allow yourselves to be shaken [1:23].

Colossians: We will. We will. *(Rises to go as Nuisances 1, 2, and 3 enter SR.)*

Nuisances 1, 2, and 3: *(Singing)* We're here again.

Colossians: *(Enormous roar)* Push off!!

(Pause. Nuisances look askance at each other.)

Nuisances 1, 2, and 3: *(Singing)* We're going again.

(Colossians roars again at them and throws the toilet roll at them as they push and shove to exit SR, obviously unnerved by this newly found confidence and assurance. Colossians turns to Paul and gives the thumbs up, which Paul returns, then exits confidently SL. Corinthians swaggers in SL and checks in at reception, apparently certain that the Receptionist is rather keen on his good looks.)

Receptionist: Dr. Paul, Corinthians is here.

Dr. Paul: Thank you, Kyrie.

Corinthians: *(Swaggers over to Paul's desk, grabs a chair, sits, puts feet up on desk, and places hands behind head.)* Hi, doc. I'm here. So what's the big news? *(Commences cleaning fingernails or being otherwise distracted.)*

Dr. Paul: Now, Corinthians, I've already had you in here once about this, but it's obvious you needed to be called in again.

Corinthians: Look, Paul old pal, this is a waste of time.

Dr. Paul: It's your personal hygiene that is the problem.

Corinthians: *(Pulled up short and highly offended)* What? How dare you!

Dr. Paul: *(Continuing)* Now I've already warned you about working together with evildoers, and I told you to avoid anything unclean [2 Corinthians 6:14]. And now look at you.

Corinthians: Look, Paul, I don't need you as my apostolic psychiatrist. I'm doing fine. My members often speak in tongues. There are lots in my congregation. And I've got some great speakers—better than you! *(Rises to go.)*

Dr. Paul: Well, reports I have heard don't agree.

Corinthians: *(Stops.)* What reports?

Dr. Paul: Some people from Chloe's family have told me quite plainly that there are quarrels among you. Each one of you says something different. One says, "I follow Paul"; another says, "I follow Apollos"; another says, "I follow Peter"; and another says, "I follow Christ." Christ has been divided into groups. Was it Paul who died for you on the cross? [1 Corinthians 1:11-13]

Corinthians: *(Waving it aside)* Those are minor hassles.

Dr. Paul: Oh really? What about the legal disputes within your congregation—Christian suing Christian before heathen judges. The very fact that you have legal disputes among yourselves shows that you have failed completely [1 Corinthians 6:4-7].

Corinthians: Well, some people like to—

Dr. Paul: *(Unabated)* Furthermore, when you meet together as a group for Communion, as you eat, each one goes ahead with his own meal; so that some are hungry and some are even getting drunk! What do you expect me to say about this? Shall I praise you? Of course I won't! [1 Corinthians 11:21-22]

Corinthians: Well, there are only a few—

Dr. Paul: *(Continuing and getting hotter)* Now it is being said that there is sexual immorality among you so terrible even the heathen would not be guilty of it. I am told a man is sleeping with his own father's second wife! How then can you be proud? The man who has done this thing should be expelled from your congregation [1 Corinthians 5:1-2].

Corinthians: We can sort all that out.

Dr. Paul: It all points to a lack of discipline and of real love [1 Corinthians 9:25; 16:14].

Corinthians: Discipline? Look, mister, we have people who speak in tongues and people who—

Dr. Paul: So what? I may be able to speak in tongues of men and even of angels, but if I have no love, my speech is nothing more than a noisy gong or a clanging bell. I may have the gift of inspired preaching, I may have all knowledge, I may have faith enough to move mountains, but if I have no love, then I am nothing. These three remain: faith, hope, and love—and the greatest of these is love [1 Corinthians 13:1-3, 8, 13].

Corinthians: *(Finally leaning on the desk)* Look, Paul. We've outgrown you. I've got my own apostles, great speakers who are better than you. The first time you came to us, you were weak and incompetent. Our speakers argued you into the ground. I'm doing fine. So don't give me this—

(Dr. Paul, who has been seething all the while, suddenly leaps to his feet and explodes.)

Dr. Paul: Now, you listen to me! This is the *second* time I've had to speak to you! You'd better not make it necessary for me to get you in a *third* time! [2 Corinthians 13:1-3] Don't force me to be harsh on you. The weapons we use in our fight are not of this world. They are God's powerful weapons which we use to destroy false arguments [2 Corinthians 10:1-5].

(He advances around the desk on Corinthians, who is completely deflated by this unexpected strength and starts to back step.)

Dr. Paul: I'm not inferior to those so-called apostles of yours [2 Corinthians 11:5]. Those men are not true apostles, they are false apostles who lie about their work and disguise themselves. I'm warning you now, and I've said it before, next time I get you in here *(jabs Corinthians in the chest)* nobody will escape punishment! [2 Corinthians 13:2]

(As Paul is saying these lines, he is backing Corinthians right 'round the desk, poking him in the chest. The final jab in the chest pushes him backward so that he falls into Paul's chair.)

Dr. Paul: And get out of my chair!

Corinthians: *(All bluster gone, Corinthians leaps out of chair, dusts it off, then stands back to allow Paul to sit.)* All right, OK. You're right. I *have* got problems. I'll...I'll try to sort them out. Honest, I will. I'll clean up. You'll see. *(Rips shirt front open and calls down into it.)* Where's that man who's been sleeping with his stepmother? Get out of me. Go on. Where are those drunken, depraved types? Get out! Get out! *(Starts to beat self.)*

Dr. Paul: *(Calming Corinthians)* All right, all right now. That's enough. It is enough that this person has been punished by most of you in this way. Now, however, you should forgive him so that he does not give up altogether [2 Corinthians 2:6-7]. I'm not sorry I was harsh on you, for it has made you change your ways, and this change of heart leads to salvation. There is no regret in that [2 Corinthians 7:8-10].

Corinthians: *(Genuine)* Thanks, doc. We'll really forge ahead now. We feel better already, *(down shirt front)* don't we?

Dr. Paul: *(Shakes hand.)* Good for you, buddy.

(Corinthians exits. Hebrews crawls in, dressed in a diaper and sucking a pacifier. He or she crawls right over to Paul, climbs up on his knee, and sits there sucking thumb.)

Receptionist: *(Running over)* I'm sorry, doctor. It's Hebrews. He (she) crawled in under the desk. I didn't see him (her).

Dr. Paul: That's fine, Kyrie. I'll handle it. *(Receptionist returns to desk.)* Hebrews, what's going on? This is ridiculous.

(Dr. Paul tries to get Hebrews off his knee, but Hebrews just clings tighter and goos.)

Dr. Paul: Stop that baby rubbish! *(Puts Hebrews on the floor.)* You're too old for that. Now go sit in that chair and talk sensibly.

Hebrews: *(Taking chair)* Doctor, you've got to help me. I can't face life anymore. It's too hard for me. I want to run away from it all and hide. *(Breaking down)* I want to get into my little cot and sleep. I haven't got any of the confidence or courage or energy that I used to have, and God probably doesn't like me anymore. Oh, where's teddy? *(Blubbers on.)*

Dr. Paul: Sounds like a dietary problem to me. What have you been eating lately in the way of spiritual food and Christian teaching?

Hebrews: Well, for breaky there was hot milk.

Dr. Paul: *(Taking notes)* Yes.

Hebrews: And for lunchy bunchy there was a milkshake.

Dr. Paul: Yes.

Hebrews: And for dinsy winsy there was…

Dr. Paul: Milk?

Hebrews: No. Custard.

Dr. Paul: What's that?

Hebrews: A milk dessert.

Dr. Paul: Don't you eat anything solid?

Hebrews: *(Horrified)* Solid? But that means I have to chew!

Dr. Paul: Well, you can chew!

Hebrews: *(Breaking down again)* Noooooo! I'm only little.

Dr. Paul: Well no wonder you're lacking vigor and maturity. No wonder you've been regressing back to babyhood. There has been enough time for you to be a leader and a teacher, yet you still need someone to teach you the first lessons of God's message. Instead of eating solid food, you still have to drink milk! Anyone who has to drink milk is still a child. Go forward, then, to mature teaching and leave behind the first lessons of the Christian message! [Hebrews 5:12–6:1]

Hebrews: You mean I should grow up?

Dr. Paul: Precisely. Look at all the great ones of the faith, all the big names. They're listed in chapter 11 of your personal church treatment plan. They didn't give up. They went *on* to bigger and better things! Remember how it was in the old days. In those days after God's light had shone on you, you suffered many things, yet you were not beaten [10:32-35].

Hebrews: *(Reminiscing)* Yeah, they were good days. I used to feel so strong and capable.

Dr. Paul: Well then, rid yourself of anything that gets in the way, and go on to run with determination the race before you. Keep your eyes on Jesus on whom your faith depends from beginning to end. Think of what he went through. Don't let yourselves be discouraged and give up [12:1-4]. And get your teeth into some good solid teaching and spiritual food to strengthen your faith.

Hebrews: Faith?

Dr. Paul: Yes, faith. To have faith is to be sure of the things we hope for, to be certain of the things we cannot see [11:1].

Hebrews: But how will we know God is with us? How can we talk to God? I need some sort of high priest to talk to God for me.

Dr. Paul: We have a great high priest who has gone into the very presence of God—Jesus, the Son of God. So let's be brave, then, and approach God's throne. There we will receive mercy and grace to help us just when we need it [4:14-16].

Hebrews: Thanks, doc. You're a saint.

Dr. Paul: *(Embarrassed)* Oh, well, you know…

(Hebrews exits SL, and Paul rises and packs briefcase.)

Dr. Paul: Right. Now, there's only the house call on Galatians to make.

(He exits SL, and there is a blackout or some form of scene change. Receptionist exits also. Lights come up to reveal Galatians lying on what was originally Paul's desk which has now become Galatians' sick bed. He is mostly covered with a sheet and lies there, groaning.)

Galatians: Oh. I feel awful.

(Judaizers 1, 2, and 3 enter SR.)

Judaizer 1: Aha!

Judaizer 2: *(Condescendingly)* Hello, Galatians.

Judaizer 3: We're back again.

Galatians: Oh, no! Not you again. Please go away!

Judaizer 1: Oh, no. That would never do. It's because we're concerned for you that we're here in the first place.

Galatians: But—

Judaizer 2: We're members of your own congregation. You can't get rid of us.

Judaizer 3: And don't think Dr. Paul can save you. He might have been OK while you were being born, but we know better than he does now.

Judaizer 1: And it's because we know better that we can tell you without the slightest shred of doubt, that…

Judaizers 1, 2, and 3: …you aren't a proper Christian!

Galatians: But—

Judaizer 2: You can't be a proper Christian unless you become a Jew first. You have to obey the Mosaic law—*(deliberately)* every little bit of it.

Galatians: But what about the grace of Jesus?

Judaizer 3: The Law is the Law, and it can't be contradicted. *(Majestically)* It stands forever!

Galatians: But—

Judaizer 1: And that means *(threateningly)* you have to be circumcised.

Galatians: What?

(Judaizers 1, 2, and 3 all bring out huge axes, knives, chain saws.)

Galatians: *(In a panic as they advance on him)* Nooo! Nooo! Help, Dr. Paul!

Dr. Paul: *(Enters SL.)* What's going on here?

(Judaizers 1, 2, and 3 retire to USR but still look threatening.)

Galatians: *(With relief)* Oh, Dr. Paul. I'm so glad you're here. They say I'm not saved anymore because I haven't been…you know…done. I don't feel like a Christian anymore. They have such good arguments *(furtive glance at Judaizers)* and such sharp instruments.

Dr. Paul: *(Taking Galatians to task)* Galatians! I am surprised at you. In no time at all you are deserting the one who called you by the grace of Christ, and are accepting another gospel. There *is* no other gospel [Galatians 1:6-7]. You foolish Galatians! Who put a spell on you? Tell me one thing: Did you receive God's Spirit by doing what the Law requires or by hearing the Gospel and believing it? *(Galatians is abashed.)* How can you be so foolish? Did all your experience mean nothing to you? [3:1-4]

Galatians: Well, I suppose, um…

Dr. Paul: We know that a person is put right with God only by faith in Jesus Christ, never by doing what the Law demands [2:16].

(Galatians repeats the last part of previous line along with Paul as if remembering it.)

Dr. Paul: See? You do remember it. Now get it in here! *(Slaps Galatians on the chest.)*

Galatians: I see it now. You mean, kind of…it is no longer I who live, but Christ who lives in me? [2:20]

Dr. Paul: Good one!

Galatians: This life that I now live, I live by faith in the Son of God, who loved me…

Dr. Paul: …and gave his life for you [2:20].

Galatians: If a person was put right with God through the Law, it would mean that Christ…

Dr. Paul: …died for nothing. Exactly! [2:21]

(Judaizers 1, 2, and 3 gulp audibly, look at their sharp instruments, drop them, and exit SR in panic.)

Galatians: *(Climbing out of bed and stretching)* I feel much better now. We feel so much more sure of ourselves.

Dr. Paul: Good. Work together. Cooperate.

Galatians: We will. After all, we are free of the Law now, so that means we can do anything we like.

Dr. Paul: Well, wait a minute. You were called to be free, but do not let this freedom become an excuse for letting your desires control you. Instead, let love make you serve one another. For the whole Law is summed up in one commandment: Love your neighbor as yourself [5:13-14]. Help carry one another's burdens, and in this way you will obey the law of Christ [6:2].

Galatians: We will. We've got a good future now.

(Galatians exits SL.)

Dr. Paul: *(To self)* Well, what a day! I should write up all these case histories one day. They'd make a great church counselor's manual. I'd call it "Weird Churches I Have Known." *(To audience)* So be alert, stand firm in the faith, be brave, be strong. Do all your work in love [1 Corinthians 16:13-14]. And may the grace of the Lord Jesus be with you all [Philemon 1:25].

(Nods decisively and smiles at audience. Exit SL. Curtain.)

Getting Through to God

Themes: Prayer, persistence, faith, Christian privilege, God's omnipresence

Summary: This skit depicts what prayer might be like if getting through to God were not just a matter of praying directly to him. It shows what it would be like if getting through to God were as difficult as it is to get through to some members of the bureaucracy.

Scripture Links: 2 Samuel 22:7; Psalm 46:1; 130:1-2; Luke 11:1-13; 18:1-8; Ephesians 6:18; Hebrews 4:14-16

Discussion Ideas: Isn't it a privilege to pray? Discussion concerning this drama may center on the amazing concept that we tiny beings are able to access directly, at any time, the omnipotent Creator of the cosmos, who *wants* us to talk to and listen to him. There is no extended chain of command or extensive bureaucracy to go through. There are no waiting lists or prerequisites. We do not rely on complex hierarchies or high priesthoods to get through for us. We have a direct and open line to God and back. It is something we take for granted far too much and because of this, it bears discussion to ensure that we *don't* take it so much for granted.

If necessary, the Arthur Christian part can be divided into two parts to reduce the line load on any one person. The director can decide how to divide the part and create some interesting interplay between the two friends as first one, then the other, makes attempt after unsuccessful attempt to contact the Deity. The part of Arthur could also be played by a female (Anne Christian), and the interplay between the female lead and some of the other characters could be modified accordingly.

Props: You'll need a table; a telephone; a small sign saying, "Talk to God. Ring 777"; and a tape recording of chimes or schmaltzy "elevator" music. (A small xylophone could be used instead to provide the sound of chimes over the telephone.) You'll also need a tape recording of the sound effects described on page 65.

Preparation: The stage can be fairly empty. There is no need to use complicated screens or hangings. Put a table DSC with a telephone on it. From the table hang a small sign saying, "Talk to God. Ring 777." Provide offstage sound effects by using taped music played over the public-address system or a small xylophone.

During the intervals of "being put through," play music over the audio system, or play those accursed chimes that some phone systems put on while you're waiting. To drive the audience even crazier, make the chimes louder and more insistent as the drama unfolds and Arthur is forced to wait again and again.

Cast of Characters

Arthur Christian (casually dressed)

Offstage voices of

Switchboard 1 (overly helpful and sugary nice)

Switchboard 2 (nasal and bored)

Snag (tough and curt)

David Spiffing (terribly efficient)

Patrick O'Dear (very Irish)

Dr. Angelbrain (German, guttural, and eccentric)

Jeb (slow, lazy, and drawly)

Well-Known Local Identity (such as a youth leader, minister, or politician)

Secretary 1 (smooth, attractive female voice)

Dag (silly, incapable of doing anything right)

Gossip 1

Gossip 2

Secretary 2 (slightly dazed as in one who has just awakened from a long sleep)

Office Clerk (only just awakened)

Mr. Doright (deep; well-rounded; masculine, once awake)

Taped Voice

God's Secretary (friendly)

God (authoritative)

Script

Getting Through to God

Arthur Christian: *(Enters SL and wanders along until he gets to table, where he stops and reads sign.)* Wow! Talk to God, eh? Right. This will be worthwhile. *(Picks up phone and rings the number.)*

Switchboard 1: Hello, Heaven Information Center. May I help you?

Arthur Christian: Yes, I'd like to talk to God, please.

Switchboard 1: I'll put you through.

Switchboard 2: Hello, Communications.

Arthur Christian: Hello, I'd like to talk to God.

Switchboard 2: Is this a prayer request?

Arthur Christian: Well, I just wanted—

Switchboard 2: Request or praise?

Arthur Christian: Well, I just wanted to talk to God. I suppose it's a bit of both.

Switchboard 2: I'll put you through to Requests.

Arthur Christian: But what if I want to thank him, too?

Switchboard 2: Then you'll have to speak to the Praise Department. Hold the line, please.

Arthur Christian: *(Aside)* Oh well, I suppose I can praise him afterward.

(Music or chimes ring out over the sound system and then suddenly stop.)

David Spiffing: Hello, Prayer Requests Department. David Spiffing here.

Arthur Christian: Oh, hello, I'd like to speak to God please.

David Spiffing: Fine. You're name is…

Arthur Christian: Arthur Christian.

David Spiffing: Right, and your address?

Arthur Christian: Fifty-five Earthly Avenue…*(insert name of local community)*.

David Spiffing: Excellent. We'll send a form to you as soon as possible. 'Bye. *(Click.)*

Arthur Christian: Hello? Hello? I just wanted to talk to…*(Dials furiously.)*

Snag: *(Tough and curt)* Hello, Heaven.

Arthur Christian: Er, hello. I wanted to speak to God, but I got cut off.

Snag: Well, that's not my fault!

Arthur Christian: Well, can you get me through?

Snag: What department do you want?

Arthur Christian: Er, Prayer Department?

Snag: No such thing!

Arthur Christian: Er…well, I think I had…

Snag: Make up your mind!

Arthur Christian: I think it was Requests.

Snag: Well, I'll try to connect you, but it's a lot of trouble—a *lot* of trouble. *(Pausing)* Line's busy; you'll have to wait. *(Music or chimes.)*

Arthur Christian: I'm awfully sorry if—

(Music or chimes cut out.)

Patrick O'Dear: Hello, Prayer Requests, Patrick O'Dear speaking.

Arthur Christian: Hello, I'd like to speak to David Spiffing.

Patrick O'Dear: He's not here. He's the head of the department.

Arthur Christian: But I was speaking to him just before.

Patrick O'Dear: That's because this is my office, and he was just in here for a minute to get some more paper clips. How may I help you?

Arthur Christian: Well, I wanted to speak to God, not write to him, just speak.

Patrick O'Dear: Well, he's very busy, so you'll have to book a call through our office. What did you want to talk about?

Arthur Christian: Oh well, it's a bit personal.

Patrick O'Dear: *(Immediate change)* Oh! Oh, that's different. Look, I'm sorry. I didn't realize—

Arthur Christian: Oh, no, it's not that personal—

Patrick O'Dear: No, please. Just the mention that it's personal is enough. We pride ourselves on confidentiality in this office.

Arthur Christian: But it's not—

Patrick O'Dear: We get all sorts of incredible personal hassles coming through here: psychopaths, sadomasochists, weirdos. You're probably just another one of those—

Arthur Christian: No, I'm not—really.

Patrick O'Dear: I'll just put you through to our Distressed and Twisted Requests section, and they'll give you sympathetic psychological counseling.

Arthur Christian: No, wait—

(Click and a couple of seconds of music or chimes.)

Dr. Angelbrain: *(German accent if it can be managed clearly.)* Hello, Dr. Angelbrain here.

Arthur Christian: Oh, doctor, it's all a bit confused.

Dr. Angelbrain: Now just relax, and take it slowly.

Arthur Christian: No, I don't want to talk to you—

Dr. Angelbrain: Of course you don't, but it's taken real guts to face up to your problem.

Arthur Christian: *(Getting annoyed)* But I don't have a problem.

Dr. Angelbrain: Now, now, don't lose touch with reality.

Arthur Christian: *(More annoyed)* Look, all I want to do is talk to God, and this stupid system has messed it all up!

Dr. Angelbrain: Yes, yes. Sometimes we all feel helpless against the system. But we have to—

Arthur Christian: *(Really angry now)* Stop it! I don't have a problem!

Dr. Angelbrain: That's it. Release all your violent tendencies. We've made some real progress here today. So I'll mail out some sedatives and a copy of my latest book entitled *Perhaps Confusion Is Not a Bad Thing.*

Arthur Christian: Wait...

Dr. Angelbrain: Give your name and address to the switchboard operator.

Arthur Christian: No—

(Click and music or chimes.)

Switchboard 1: Hello, Switch.

Arthur Christian: Hello, I still want to speak to God.

Switchboard 1: Requests or Praise?

Arthur Christian: Requests.

Switchboard 1: Connecting.

Jeb: *(Broad, sloppy accent)* 'Ullo.

Arthur Christian: Hello, I want to talk to God or anyone who can put me in contact with God.

Jeb: You'd have to speak to the director. *(Pause.)*

Arthur Christian: Well, can I?

Jeb: Nope. He's out to lunch.

Arthur Christian: Then get me David Spiffing.

Jeb: He's away at a conference for the rest of the week.

Arthur Christian: Well, when will the director be back?

Jeb: He's usually back by now, so he should be here any minute.

Arthur Christian: Can he get me through?

Jeb: For requests only, yes.

Arthur Christian: I'll wait.

Jeb: Whatever you like. *(Hangs up.)*

Arthur Christian: No, no, I'll wait on the phone. Aargh!

(Dials furiously again.)

Well-Known Local Identity: *(Minister, youth group leader, politician, or some highly placed and very fierce person.)* Hello, _____ here.

Arthur Christian: *(Gulps.)* Sorry. Wrong number. *(Hangs up and dials again.)* Hello, I want to speak to the Director of Prayer Requests.

Switchboard 2: I'll put you through to his secretary.

Arthur Christian: *(Exploding)* No, not his secretary! I don't want to speak to his secretary or his deputy, just him!

Secretary 1: Hello, Director's office. May I help you?

Arthur Christian: *(Immediate change as the voice is obviously that of an extremely sophisticated and attractive young lady)* Oh, oh hello. I was wanting to speak to the Director, but you'll do nicely.

Secretary 1: *(Giggles.)* Oh, thanks, you naughty thing, you.

Arthur Christian: Actually, what are you doing this Friday night?

Secretary 1: Well, actually I'm free, but, look, I'll just change phones. This one has been cutting out a bit recently and—*(Click.)*

Arthur Christian: Hello. Hello? Rats! *(Dials furiously. Click.)*

Arthur Christian: Hi, honey, about Friday night—

Snag: How dare you talk to me like that!

Arthur Christian: *(Shellshocked)* Oh, sorry. I wanted the Secretary of Prayer Requests, please.

Snag: This *is* the Secretary of Prayer Requests.

Arthur Christian: *(Pitifully)* But what happened to the nice young lady?

Snag: She's the morning secretary. I just came on shift. Now state your business or get off the line, you weirdo!

Arthur Christian: *(Nervously explaining)* Oh, well, I wanted to speak to God, and they told me that the Director of Prayer Requests could help me and that he'd be back from lunch any minute. Is he back yet? Can I speak to him?

Snag: No, you can't. He got back three minutes ago, and he has since left.

Arthur Christian: Well, when will he be back?

Snag: He's gone on six months' vacation.

Arthur Christian: Can I call him at home?

Snag: He's staying in a Tibetan monastery for the whole six months.

Arthur Christian: Oh no!

Snag: Oh yes, and it serves you right!

Arthur Christian: *(Hopelessly)* Can you put me back to the switchboard, please?

Snag: All right, but it's a lot of trouble—a *lot* of trouble.

(Music or chimes.)

Switchboard 1: Hello, Switch.

Arthur Christian: Hello, I want to speak to God.

Switchboard 1: Requests or Praise?

Arthur Christian: *(Leaps.)* Praise! Praise! Don't put me through to Requests!

Switchboard 1: I'll put you through.

(Music or chimes.)

Dag: *(A really silly voice that bespeaks limited ability to understand anything at all)* Hello, Praise Department.

Arthur Christian: Hello, I want to speak to God. *(Silence.)* Well, can you help me?

Dag: No, well, not really. The man you want is the Regional Praise

Coordinator, but he's away. But his deputy could help you.

Arthur Christian: Can I speak to him, then?

Dag: No, he's away too.

Arthur Christian: Is there anyone who can put me through?

Dag: Well, they're all away at a staff training seminar. They all have to be facilitated. I'm the only one here.

Arthur Christian: Can *you* put me through?

Dag: Well, I only just started here the other day, so I'm not sure how this system works. I'll try. Name, please.

Arthur Christian: Arthur Christian.

Dag: Slower, please.

Arthur Christian: *(Steadily)* Arthur Christian.

Dag: Spell, please.

Arthur Christian: C-h-r-i-s-t-...

Dag: No, the first name.

Arthur Christian: A-r-t-h-...

Dag: Slower, please.

Arthur Christian: *(Painfully with gritted teeth)* A-r-t-h-u-r! There, got it?

Dag: Um...yes...no...oh, it's no use trying to remember it. I'll have to write it down.

Arthur Christian: *(Exploding)* Look! Can I speak to anyone else in the Praise Section?

Dag: No, I'm the only one...hold on, there's a light on in Mr. Doright's office.

Arthur: Who's he?

Dag: He's the official, acting, assistant, undersection submanager. He's in charge of departmental efficiency.

Arthur Christian: Well, put me through to him.

Dag: All right. Now, let me see, how does this thing work?

(Clicks and assorted sound effects followed by the sound of a radio coming on and off again with music, weather, or news. Then a crossed wire occurs.)

Gossip 1: And I said to him, I've never been so insulted in all my life.

Gossip 2: Good for you, dear, and what did he say? *(Click.)*

Dag: Hello. I'm still trying.

Arthur Christian: You certainly are!

Dag: Oh, here it is. *(Click. Voice of Dag is replaced by loud background snoring sounds from several people sounding like a hogs' slumber party.)*

Arthur Christian: *(After waiting a bit)* Er, hello.

Secretary 2: *(Obviously jumping)* Oh! Oh, yes, er…*(Mad scrambling for the phone. Background snores continue.)* Hello, Mr. Doright's office.

Arthur Christian: *(Steadily, trying to control mounting frustration)* Hello. Can I speak to Mr. Doright, please?

Secretary 2: *(With a hint of panic)* Oh, er, yes, certainly. I'll put you through.

(There is a thump as the phone is put down and more mad scramblings in the background.)

Secretary 2: *(Loudly whispering in the background)* Wake him up. Quick, wake him up.

Office Clerk: Quick, wake up, Mr. Doright!

(Both Secretary and Office Clerk go into a mad flap, trying to rouse Mr. Doright, who is still snoring blissfully.)

Mr. Doright: *(Snores cut out with a snort. Dopily)* Go away.

Secretary 2: It's the phone. Someone's on the phone!

Office Clerk: The phone, the phone. Quick.

Mr. Doright: Eh, what? Oh, yes, of course. Hello.

Secretary 2: No, not that one. The one over there.

(The voice when it comes is deep, official, and confident.)

Mr. Doright: Ahem. Yes. Hello. John Doright here.

Arthur Christian: *(Pouring heart out)* Look, I've had an awful time. I only want to speak to God. I've been led around for hours by the Prayer Requests Department. No one seems to be able to do anything right. Can't anyone get me through to God?

Mr. Doright: Ah, yes, I sympathize. The Prayer Requests mob are a bunch of incompetent bumblers. Couldn't organize an ice factory at the South Pole. Look, the fellow you want is the Permanent Head of the Individual Praise Prayers Office. He'll cut the red tape and put you straight through. I'd do it myself, but I…er…have some urgent work to do. *(Outburst of clandestine laughter and mock agreement from staff in background which is noisily shushed by Mr. Doright.)* Ahem…I'll put you through to the IPP office direct.

Arthur Christian: *(Tears of gratitude)* Thanks a lot. You have no idea what I've been through.

Mr. Doright: No problem at all. Hold the line. *(In the background)* I thought

I told you to take the phone off the hook.

(A mumbled apology from someone is cut off by click and music or chimes then a click and ominous silence.)

Arthur Christian: *(Cautiously)* Hello, is this the Head of the Individual Praise Prayers Office?

Dag: Hello. Yes, it is.

Arthur Christian: *(Exploding)* Not you again! What are you doing there?

Dag: *(Happily)* I got promoted. May I help you please?

(There is a click and the Taped Voice comes on in bored tones.)

Taped Voice: This is a *(insert name of local telecommunications company)* announcement. The number you were dialing has been disconnected due to nonpayment of fees. To speak to God, now call 000 777.

(Arthur grits his teeth and dials furiously.)

God's Secretary: Hello. God's office. Secretary speaking.

Arthur Christian: *(Breathing heavily and on verge of insanity)* Hello. I want to speak to God, now, urgent! I don't want to write to him, and I don't want to speak to anyone else. Just him. Just for a minute! OK?

God's Secretary: Well, God is very busy. You'll have to be brief.

Arthur Christian: *(Pulling at hair in frustration)* I'll be brief!

God's Secretary: I'll put you through. When God answers, speak clearly, and state your name and business in thirty seconds. No extended lists of names or incidents.

Arthur Christian: Anything. *Anything!* Just put me through!

God's Secretary: Connecting.

(There is the usual insistent music or chimes as Arthur waits with his adrenaline and frustration levels rising out of control. He writhes, sweats, and squirms until finally the answer comes.)

God: Hello, God here.

(But Arthur has lost it. Mouth agape, eyes staring, he can only emit a choking gurgle.)

God: Hello?

Arthur Christian: I...I...*(Bursts out.)* I can't remember what I was going to say!

God: Try ringing back later. 'Bye.

(With the final click, Arthur emits a piercing shriek, and there is a blackout.)

Excuses, Excuses

Themes: Taking responsibility for decisions, reasons to believe, outreach, seeking the truth, excuses

Summary: A lifelong "seeker of truth" is confronted by the truth of the Gospel and reacts with great discomfort as he or she realizes the ramifications of that truth.

Scripture Links: Matthew 7:13-14; 8:18-22; 10:37-39; 11:25-30; 19:16-30; Mark 4:1-20

Discussion Ideas: This is a good skit to use for a seeker service or as an outreach tool. It is also good for eliciting a discussion about apologetics. The skit prompts discussion about the ways and reasons people try to dodge the Gospel and the fact that it can be a scary thing to some people because of its ability to cause radical change.

Props: You'll need a table, a Bible, a pen, and paper.

Preparation: Place a table DSR, and set some paper and a pen on it.

Cue

Because this skit contains quite a few lines for two actors to learn, consider dividing the Searcher part into two parts and the Gospel part into two parts: the New Testament and Old Testament, and simply calling it Bible, rather than Gospel. You will need to modify a couple of lines in the first section when the Gospel is introducing itself to the Searcher. With four characters running to and fro on the stage, trying to escape and pursue, you should be able to work out some very good movement stunts and gags. Walk it through as you read the lines, and you will be amazed at the funny ideas that come into your head.

Cast of Characters

Searcher (somewhat grandiose and overconfident; dressed in ordinary clothes)

Gospel (earnest and energetic; dressed in ordinary clothes)

Script

Excuses, Excuses

Searcher: *(Enters SL with various dramatic gestures and balletic movements.)* I am a searcher. I seek wisdom, truth, and ultimately God. I search the heights. I search the depths. My life has been a quest. Where, oh, where are wisdom, truth, and God? I have been to the heights of the Himalayan peaks and meditated. I have secluded myself amid the vast deserts of the mystic Arabian east. I have sifted the mysteries of the tarot cards and Ouija board. I have studied volumes in university libraries—on history, philosophy, art, science. I have delved into the very bowels of the literary masterpieces of East and West, but still my mind wanders in restless search for wisdom, truth, and God. *(Reaching a peak of emotion)* Oh, wisdom—where hidest thee? Oh, God—I desire to find thee. Oh, truth—where concealest thou thee?

Gospel: *(Enters SR.)* Here I am.

Searcher: *(Starts and looks over shoulder.)* Eh? Who are you?

Gospel: I'm the Gospel.

Searcher: The who?

Gospel: The Gospel. The good news.

Searcher: About what?

Gospel: The good news about Jesus Christ.

Searcher: But hold on. I don't quite see how this all connects. I say I'm searching for wisdom, truth, and God, and you tell me you're the good news about Jesus Christ. I mean, where's the link?

Gospel: Well, you've heard of Jesus Christ, as in the Bible.

Searcher: My dear, I have studied the Bible at the university level. I did three years on ancient Near Eastern literature.

Gospel: Well, it's not just literature. In it is the good news about Jesus Christ.

Searcher: Look, I'm a *(more dramatic gestures)* searcher, a struggler, taking joy in the pleasure of the hunt, forever seeking the elusive…

Gospel: *(Following after)* That's what I'm saying. Here is what you've been looking for. The Gospel is the truth and wisdom of God. It's God speaking to us. You don't need to seek God anymore. God has come looking for you. Your search is over.

Searcher: *(Stops dead.)* Eh?

Gospel: Your search is over.

Searcher: *(Deflates.)* Oh.

Gospel: Here. *(Holds out Bible.)* Look. Listen. Feel. Open your heart and mind to take it in. It's more than just literature. It's God calling your name. *(Gospel holds Bible out and walks toward Searcher, but Searcher deftly avoids Gospel.)*

Searcher: Oh, come on. A book thousands of years old? Is that relevant to today's modern, high-tech society?

Gospel: Well, you are the one who sifted the tarot cards and Ouija board. How high-tech is that?

Searcher: *(Hadn't thought of that one.)* Well…

Gospel: Anyway, of course it's relevant. Look, if there really is a loving God behind this whole universe, won't that make a huge difference to the way you feel about yourself and life and everything?

Searcher: I suppose…

Gospel: Won't it mean you will value yourself and other people more because you are all creations of a loving God?

Searcher: Yes, but…

Gospel: And if Jesus was God on earth, showing us how we can live forever in happiness with our ultimate Parent, isn't that the most important fact you could ever deal with?

Searcher: Yes, I see that, but er…*(Backs away from Gospel.)* Jesus? That's Christianity. That's a religion. I'm not the religious sort.

Gospel: *(Laughs.)* There's no such thing as the religious sort. That's a myth. All types of people respond to the Gospel—athletes, academics, professionals, tradespeople, even…*(Insert name of a well-known local team or group.)*

Searcher: But, religion! I mean, such terrible things have been done in the name of religion.

Gospel: Yes, and also in the names of science and medicine and art. Can I help it if some power-hungry politician corrupts the Gospel message and uses it for his own ends? Here. *(Holds Bible out.)* Take it. You don't have to go on struggling. *(Puts it in Searcher's hand.)*

Searcher: *(Looks at it, then returns it.)* I have some questions to ask first.

Gospel: Fire away. I have a very rational side to me as well as the mystery.

Searcher: Well, er...you have to understand that I'm not prepared just to take it on blind faith. That's like believing in Santa Claus.

Gospel: Well, study it. Investigate the evidence. Faith doesn't rest on nothing. It's built on evidence, facts that you weigh up first.

Searcher: Yeah, but you can't prove that there is a God.

Gospel: And you can't prove that someone loves you. Or that you are alive. Or that you are the same person you were five minutes ago. All you can do is go on the evidence and make a reasonable decision.

Searcher: What evidence?

Gospel: Well, the fact that the world exists. The fact that it shows design and purpose. The fact that you have a distinct personality, a conscience, a sense of values. The fact that all humans everywhere have a sense of worship.

Searcher: But how can you scientifically demonstrate—

Gospel: Look, the basic assumption behind all science is that there is order and sanity in the universe. Otherwise all scientific theories and laws go out the window. They all rely on a reasonable, predictable universe, and a rational universe is not the type of thing you'd expect if there were nothing but chaos and chance behind it.

Searcher: But the Gospel stories are too airy-fairy.

Gospel: They're not. They are grounded in actual historical events. Documents verify them. You can study them. It's not in some mystical legendary past age. *(Walks across to give Bible, but Searcher dodges again.)*

Searcher: Well, explain all the evil in the world.

Gospel: Well, explain all the good in the world. It's only belief in a loving God who hates evil that keeps us from going insane or becoming totally callous.

Searcher: *(Desperately races to table.)* But...I still have objections. *(Grabs paper and pencil, scribbles, then holds up paper confidently.)*

Gospel: *(Reading)* "There are too many hypocrites in the church." *(Indignantly)* Aw, this is an old one.

Searcher: But I've just thought of it now.

Gospel: Rubbish. It's been used as an excuse for years.

Searcher: Well…*(Scribbles again and holds up paper.)*

Gospel: *(Reading)* "Christianity is just a crutch." Of course it is. And if you realize you are a cripple, a crutch is a good thing. It's not weakness to admit you need God. It's wisdom. Come on—wisdom—isn't that what you've been looking for? The fear of the Lord is the beginning of wisdom. It's in the book of Proverbs.

Searcher: *(Leaning on table)* But religions are all so—

Gospel: *(Getting annoyed)* Will you stop calling Christianity a religion! Christianity is a living friendship freely offered to us by God. We can't do the reaching up. God does the reaching down. That's what I said Jesus did for us. *(Pushes Bible across table to Searcher.)*

Searcher: *(Surreptitiously slips it back.)* But I'm too evil.

Gospel: *(Becoming exasperated with all the objections.)* That's the whole idea of it. Where else do you hear of a God who forgives people by taking their guilt on himself and dying in their place? Look, here I am, offering you truth, wisdom, and a relationship with God, and all you can do is make excuses.

Searcher: They're not excuses. *(Tries to race offstage past Gospel.)*

Gospel: *(Grabs Searcher as he or she goes past.)* When are you going to make a decision? Come on! The Gospel of Jesus doesn't just stand around. *(Shaking Searcher a bit)* I demand that you respond to me!

Searcher: *(Struggling)* I will…tomorrow. Tomorrow I'll make a decision.

Gospel: *(Releasing Searcher abruptly)* Then you've already made a decision. *(Searcher is surprised and doesn't try to run off.)* You've decided to put it off. Not a good start.

Searcher: *(Somewhat relieved)* It's OK. I just need some more time. *(Starts to walk off SL confidently.)*

Gospel: *(Calling after)* How do you know you've got more time? Come on. It may be now or never.

Searcher: *(He or she is almost offstage but stops dead, then begins to panic, dives over to table, and begins to scribble again, talking as he or she writes and pushing the written objections across table toward Gospel as each one is finished.)* "But I was brought up in a strict, nonreligious home." "I went to a bad school." "Some of my best friends are ministers." "My wife supports…" *(Insert name of local charity.)* "The church always asks for money."

Gospel: *(Strides over, brushes all these off the table, and leans across table to Searcher, who backs off down under table. Gospel follows relentlessly across the table on his or her stomach until Gospel is lying across table, looking under it directly into Searcher's face.)* When will you stop this nonsense and face the facts? These excuses are nothing more than smoke screens! The basic question is this: What do you think of Jesus Christ? How do you respond to his claim to be God on earth with us?

Searcher: But...

Gospel: *(Leaning further under table as Searcher inches out from under table.)* Because that's what it all boils down to. You say you want the truth. Have the courage of your convictions. Investigate me. *(Gospel passes Bible right under the table to Searcher, who is backing out. Gospel falls off table and crawls along under table, pursuing Searcher as Searcher backs further out and climbs up onto top of table. Gospel comes out from under table, stands, and holds Bible up to Searcher, who is on table.)*

Searcher: Isn't there any way I can get away from you?

Gospel: *(Lowering Bible)* Well, yes. There is. Sort of.

Searcher: *(Hopefully, getting off table)* There is? How?

Gospel: *(Simply)* Ignore me.

Searcher: You mean it? Just that? OK. *(Turns away from Gospel and waits a bit, then peeps around.)* You're still there.

Gospel: Yes.

Searcher: *(Disappointed)* You mean you won't go away?

Gospel: Nope. Not once you are aware of me. I'm in your mind now. Every time you look in the back of your memory, I'll challenge you again.

Searcher: *(Thinks, then spins round.)* Ha. I've got you. What about the heathen natives in some dark, Amazonian rain forest? They haven't heard of you. *(Poking Gospel in chest)* How will they be judged, eh?

Gospel: You're right. They haven't heard of me. And God will be perfectly fair and just with them. But you don't have to worry about them just now. They'll be fine. There's a whole different system for them. *(Poking Searcher in chest)* *You're* the problem. You *have* heard of me. And you know what I think?

Searcher: What?

Gospel: I think you're *too scared* to investigate me properly, because you might have to change and respond and get involved.

Searcher: But I'm a searcher. I love searching.

Gospel: But do you love finding? *(Holds Bible out.)*

Searcher: *(Silent, gulps, puts hand out, then stops.)* It's ticking.

Gospel: Yes. There's a time limit. *(Pausing)* Come on. It's great knowing how much God loves you.

(Searcher hesitates, puts hand out slowly toward Bible, pauses. Blackout.)

Where Am I?

Themes: Judgment, accountability, free will, life after death, sin, redemption

Summary: This skit portrays the reaction of a nonbeliever who discovers that there is life after death and that it isn't at all what was expected.

Scripture Links: Isaiah 13:9-11; Joel 2:31-32; Matthew 5:21-22; Romans 14:10-12; 2 Thessalonians 1:8-10; 2 Peter 2:4-10

Discussion Ideas: This hard-hitting drama starts comically, but its ending can leave an audience stunned, silent, and thoughtful. It is challenging and does not pull any punches in addressing the concepts of judgment and separation from God. In discussions after the skit, it is essential to deal with the implications of total separation from God because this is an idea that most people (including many Christians) studiously avoid. The topics of hell and punishment are not popular nowadays; many would prefer to believe that there is no such thing as right and wrong and that it doesn't matter what one thinks as long as one is sincere.

Props and Costumes: You will need a covered table, rubber stamps, chairs for two Receptionists, and a couple of folders full of papers. The Receptionists should be nicely dressed in office attire, but they should be wearing heavy black eye makeup to make their eyes particularly intense, almost grotesque.

Cue

If you don't have a curtain or blackout facility, conceal the Receptionists' faces behind newspapers or books at the beginning of the skit. Then, when the face of Receptionist 1 is revealed, its grotesque eyes will have a greater impact on the audience.

Preparation: Place the table DSC. Cover it to the floor with a long, dark cloth so that when the Receptionists sink behind it at the end of the skit, their feet will not be visible. Be sure to eliminate any backlighting that would reveal the Receptionists through the cloth.

Cue

The two Receptionist parts can be combined if necessary, or they can be further divided into three or even four parts.

Cast of Characters

Receptionists 1 and 2 (cold, businesslike, and condescending; dressed for office work—combinations of red and black are effective)

Script

Where Am I?

Scene: *The desk at the gate of hell. Two Receptionists are seated behind it and are occupied with various activities such as reading the paper or scribbling with their heads down so that their faces are concealed.*

Receptionist 1: *(Suddenly sitting up and looking intently at what is apparently a video screen up on the back wall behind the audience)* Oops. Look at the screen. *(Singsong)* Here comes another one.

Receptionist 2: *(Looking up)* Oh, yes. I love the looks on their faces, don't you?

Receptionist 1: *(Mirthless chuckle)* Absolutely. No idea at all what's happened. Always takes awhile to register.

Receptionist 2: It's funny how they always seem to think they're still back there, wherever they were at the end.

Receptionist 1: Yes. Takes awhile for their senses to adjust, I suppose. Anyway, let's get busy. This one'll be through the tunnel at any moment. Get the files.

Receptionist 2: No, wait. Let's try and pick it first. What do you think?

Receptionist 1: *(Studying screen closely)* Western Hemisphere?

Receptionist 2: Oh, I'd say definitely Western Hemisphere, Western culture. You can tell by the awestruck look on the face.

Receptionist 1: That's what I thought. They think they're so technological in the West. Most of them have ceased to believe in any of this stuff.

Receptionist 2: A good person, do you think?

Receptionist 1: Oh, average I'd say. Neither one nor the other. What's that term they always use when they get here?

Receptionist 2: "Well-meaning."

Receptionist 1: That's it. Well-meaning. Such a delightfully wishy-washy phrase. It could mean anything. Still, I suppose this one will have heard about *it* somewhere along the line.

Receptionist 2: Oh yes, most of them in the Western areas have. It's still sort of cultural, isn't it? I mean, it's on TV now and then, in a somewhat inaccurate form. This one probably heard about it as a child and then dropped it.

Receptionist 1: Yes, so many do. We often have to jog their memories, don't we? Er, do you think this one is…

Receptionist 2: Oh, no. I'd say definitely not. Hasn't got that air of confidence. More of a wanderer, this one. Definitely one of ours. We'll have a bit of explaining to do to this one, I should think. Oh well, here we go. *(Takes a breath.)* Get out the old rigmarole.

(They grit their teeth, hold onto the desk, and close their eyes as they brace themselves for what is obviously to be a bit of a rough arrival. The "new arrival" apparently arrives DSC in front of them, and they flinch. Because of the way the stage is set, they seem to be talking to the invisible arrival but are effectively addressing the audience.)

Receptionist 1: *(Condescendingly friendly)* Hello. Suppose you're feeling a bit on the confused side. Yes? Well, we're here to help you sort it all out.

Receptionist 2: *(Sharply)* Don't take a seat. Just stand there; that will be fine.

Receptionist 1: Where are the doctors? Yes, I thought you'd ask that.

Receptionist 2: Take it from us—the doctors are gone. You were a bit beyond them. Now, your name is…*(Pauses for answer.)* Oh, you remember, do you? Good. Do you have any idea at all where you are? *(The answer is obviously in the negative.)* No.

Receptionist 1: *(Condescendingly playful)* Well, we'll see if we can give you a little hint. It's different from where you were before, and it goes on forever and ever.

Receptionist 2: That's right. You have physically died. *(To Receptionist 1)* This one is picking it up.

Receptionist 1: Eh? Oh, no. You're not there; perish the thought. You, er, didn't make it. This is the reception area for the other one, you know, although it's probably not quite what you would expect.

(They both take files out and open them.)

Receptionist 1: Now, let's look at the—

Receptionist 2: *(Without looking up from file)* Yes, that's the name you Westerners generally use. Not a very nice name up there, so I'm told. Now let's look at the—

Receptionist 1: *(The arrival has apparently made another comment. Turns to 2.)* Oh, now isn't it amazing how many of them say that when we tell them? *(To arrival)* No, it's not a joke. This is *it*.

Receptionist 2: *(To Receptionist 1, expectantly)* I know what's going to happen now. Yes, look, there it is: pinch pinch, shake shake. It's like a little dance, isn't it?

Receptionist 1: *(Strongly, to put a stop to the nonsense)* And you're not dreaming either! *(Arrival makes another comment.)* Yes, this *can* be happening. It *is* happening.

Receptionist 2: *(Kindly)* What else do you think happens when you die as you just did? Now, enough of this. We need to— *(Annoyed response to arrival's interruption)* Oh, what is it now?

Receptionist 1: *(Exasperated)* Oh, these Westerners. They think they know it all!

Receptionist 2: Yes, we know you are an educated person. And we know you thought science had gotten rid of all this. But it didn't. Science didn't make any difference to *these* facts. Now just shut up and stop asking questions *(sharply)* and stop looking at me in that stupid, dazed fashion!

Receptionist 1: *(Shaking head in disbelief)* They just don't expect it, do they? Who knows what they teach them up there nowadays? Look, I bet I know what you're going to say next. *(Pause.)* See, told you.

Receptionist 2: Yes, we are quite aware that you have always been an "OK type of person." It's all here in the files. We don't miss a trick, you know.

(Pause and then both burst out laughing.)

Receptionist 1: There it is. Well-meaning! Oh, how I do love that expression. Look, you may have been well-meaning and even good, according to your definition of it, but our file here lists twelve and a half million little naughties, and they're all yours, right back to the age of five.

Receptionist 2: We're not allowed to count them much before that.

Receptionist 1: Yes, that's twelve and a half million! We've got them all— every dirty word, every angry thought. *(Looking at the file)* And there are some quite murderous ones here, aren't there? Yes, we know you "never *did* them," but you did *think* them. And that's not all you thought. Look at these little ideas you concocted, especially about that nice-looking person at the office where you used to work. Er, would you like me to read out the details? No? Pity. There are some good ones.

Receptionist 2: *(Continuing unabated and paging on through the files)* And then there are all the *lies*. Look at them. Mostly little white ones, but still lies. And all the things you know you should have done but you didn't, and all the bits where you got back at someone via someone else so it wouldn't look like your fault. And all the selfishness, and all the...*(turning through a few more pages)* my goodness, you've been quite busy for a well-meaning person, haven't you?

Receptionist 1: You see, they're all yours, aren't they? You seem to have a funny definition of what makes a well-meaning person. So there's no need to cop that old plea, "I don't deserve to be here," is there. Hmm?

(Fause.)

Receptionist 2: Oh, you thought you'd go *there*, did you? Well, let me tell you, that place is only for those who meet his standards, and you definitely don't. You see, *he* has very precise standards, and if you want to be with *him* and be near *him* and be in *his* place, you have to be perfect, *(shrugging)* and you just aren't.

Receptionist 1: Either that or you have to have someone else get you in there, and there's only one person who can do that. *(Checking)* And the signature just isn't on this file—

Receptionist 2: *(Jumping in)* Hold on. What's that there? *(Paging back)* I thought I just saw a word starting with J. Oh, no. Forget it. It's only the word "jealousy."

Receptionist 1: So, all the little naughties are still there, aren't they, even though most of them are "only little," as you say. None of them have been wiped out, and you can't undo them.

Receptionist 2: Oh yes, now it's all coming back, isn't it? It's the stuff you heard when you were a child, before you dropped it.

Receptionist 1: *(Paging back)* Actually, we watched you make that decision.

Receptionist 2: *(Also checking and then finding it)* Yes, here it is. Page 478. "Boring, childish fairy tale" was the term you used.

Receptionist 1: What's that? You thought *everyone* would go to heaven? *(To Receptionist 2)* I saw this one coming. *(Turning back to arrival)* Oh well, that would be a great system, wouldn't it? Yes, there they all are: all the worst villains in history. All up there, with him, happy as Larry. Oh, come on! He does have *some* sense of justice, you know! *(Pauses, listening.)* Oh, not those, eh? You mean only real baddies like thieves and muggers. Well, when does a naughty stop being a naughty, hmm? *(Indicating file)* They're all there, aren't they?

Receptionist 2: Twelve and a half million of them from age five. Or, if you want to be generous, we can take it from age twelve—that's ten and a half million.

Receptionist 1: *(To Receptionist 2)* Oh yes, here it comes. *(To arrival)* Look, you are *not* in that class. You are not a native in the depths of the Amazon rain forest who never heard about Jesus. You are from a so-called Christian, Western nation. You heard this stuff a hundred times, and you threw it all out.

Receptionist 2: As a matter of fact, *(checking file)* you went to church a few times as an adult. You even went to an adult fellowship group once, remember? *(Reading from file)* You were asked along by a friend, and you went, determined to be bored and determined to find as many things wrong with it as possible. You didn't want to make any changes in your life. Oh no! You've had plenty of chances to find out.

Receptionist 2: *(Very angry reaction to a comment from arrival)* Oh, yes, you have! You were surrounded by it. In your country there was a church on every corner, a minister on every block. You had Christians working in your office with you. They tried to tell you about it, and you never responded. You were free to go and investigate it at any time. There were no secret police sneaking about, persecuting Christians in your country. You wouldn't have been arrested and tortured for venturing into a church or reading a Christian book. Good grief! There were *shops* full of books about it; cassettes, CDs, whole libraries *available* to you. So don't you try and tell me you've never had the chance.

Receptionist 1: *(Conciliatory)* I'm sorry. The Gospel was presented to you quite fairly. You've had plenty of opportunity to respond. You don't come into the Amazon–rain forest category at all. There's a whole different system for people like that.

Receptionist 1: *(Recoils from what is obviously a cheeky comment from arrival)* Oh! Don't they get cocky! Yes, you're right. There *will* probably be heaps of your friends in there anyway. But, no, you won't be able to all "party on" together.

Receptionist 2: You won't even be able to see them. It's too dark in there, for a start. And they won't be your friends anymore anyway. You see, friendship isn't something we have in there.

Receptionist 1: Friendship is something he made up, so it's not in here. OK? *(Astonished)* Didn't you think any of this through when you were—

(Receptionist 2 nudges Receptionist 1.)

Receptionist 1: Oh yes, that's right. I forgot. "Boring, childish fairy tale." Dropped it when you were fifteen. Same old story.

Receptionist 2: Look, you really should have thought all this through for yourself. It's an ultimate issue. *(Like a teacher)* He is everything that is good and right and healthy. OK? Well, this is the place where he *isn't*. OK? He's present in the world where you were and in other places, but not in here.

Receptionist 1: So that means that nothing that has anything to do with him is around here at all. No light, no friendship, no health, happiness, love, truth, laughter, beauty, any of that stuff—

Receptionist 2: It's all totally absent.

Receptionist 1: Instead, you have all the opposites, except in a pure form—

Receptionist 2: Because there's none of him here to dilute them.

Receptionist 1: *(Reacts to objection from arrival.)* Of course, it's fair. Look, this was your own decision made a dozen times. If you didn't want to spend a life of fifty-eight years on earth with God, there's no logical way you should suddenly start wanting to be with him forever, is there?

Receptionist 2: God doesn't *force* himself on people. This is what you decided.

(Receptionist 1 and Receptionist 2 stand with an air of finality. They both take rubber stamps and heavily stamp the files.)

Receptionist 1: So there it is. I think we've about wrapped it up, don't you? *(They turn a couple of pages and stamp their files again.)*

Receptionist 2: Any final questions? *(They stamp again.)*

Receptionist 1: None? Right. That's it.

(They start to stamp one final time, but their hands seem to be frozen, and they stop in midair. They try again. The same thing happens. The stamps will not go down to the paper. Then Receptionist 1 and Receptionist 2 suddenly look at each other. They are beginning to disappear slowly down behind their desk, bending their knees slowly, ever so slightly, so that it seems they are sinking. They look at each other.)

Receptionist 1: Hey.

Receptionist 2: What?

Receptionist 1: You're fading.

Receptionist 2: *(Surprised)* Am I?

Receptionist 1: *(Bewildered)* You're getting smaller. You're fading out. Going. *(They drop their stamps.)*

Receptionist 2: Hey. Maybe we were a dream after all.

Receptionist 1: Yes, maybe we were…a dream…

(They turn to blankly face the audience, but their eyes are big, burning, intense. They are almost gone.)

Receptionist 2: A dream…

Receptionist 1: Just a dream…

Receptionist 2: *(Clearly)* This time!

(They are gone. Curtain.)